The Unreality Industry

The Unreality Industry

The Deliberate Manufacturing
of Falsehood and What It Is Doing
to Our Lives

by Ian I. Mitroff
and Warren Bennis

OXFORD UNIVERSITY PRESS
New York   Oxford

Oxford University Press

Oxford   New York   Toronto
Delhi   Bombay   Calcutta   Madras   Karachi
Kuala Lumpur   Singapore   Hong Kong   Tokyo
Nairobi   Dar es Salaam   Cape Town
Melbourne   Auckland   Madrid
and associated companies in
Berlin   Ibadan

First published in 1989 by Birch Lane Press, Carol Publishing Group
600 Madison Avenue, New York, New York 10022

First issued as an Oxford University Press paperback, 1993

Oxford is a registered trademark of Oxford University Press

Library of Congress Cataloging-in-Publication Data
Mitroff, Ian I.
    The unreality industry : the deliberate manufacturing of falsehood
and what it is doing to our lives / by Ian I. Mitroff and Warren
Bennis.
      p.   cm.
    Originally published: New York : Birch Lane Press, Carol Pub.
Group, 1989.
    Includes bibliographical references and index.
    ISBN 0-19-508398-9 (pbk.)
    1. Mass media—Social aspects—United States.   2. Popular culture—
United States.   3. Public opinion—United States.   4. Truthfulness
and falsehood.   5. Mass media—United States—Psychological aspects.
6. Knowledge, Theory of.   I. Bennis, Warren G.   II. Title.
HN90.M3M58   1993
306'.0973—dc20   92-44601

10 9 8 7 6 5 4 3

Printed in the United States of America

To our wives,
DONNA MITROFF and MARY JANE O'DONNELL

Acknowledgments

We are indebted to the following persons who read earlier portions or the entire manuscript of *The Unreality Industry* and commented on it, even though we were not always wise enough to follow their suggestions: Peter Bearse, Peter Clarke, Norman Corwin, Richard Lanham, Deana Meehan, Gary Ranker, Jay Rayvid, Everett Rogers, Dek Rosell, Deke Simon, and Firdaus Udwadia. Lastly, this book is lovingly dedicated to our wives who provide a constant, warm, and intelligent fix on reality.

Contents

4. Manufacturing People: The Prosthetic Society 71

Concerning real people who are artificial,
and artificial people who are real.

5. The Industrialized Perfection of Rottenness   90

What makes something an industry and
what does not?

6. The Culture of Unreality: Historical Roots   123

Why are we predisposed to accept
unreality?

7. The Heroless, Leaderless Society: Contemporary Roots   147

In what way have our leaders failed us?

8. The Metaphysics of Sappiness: The Primitivization of the American Intellect   169

Epilogue   196

A Fable

Notes   202

Index   213

Preface to the Paperback Edition

Try this sexual fantasy on for size: Author Howard Rheingold, who writes about the you-are-there technology known as virtual reality, predicts that consenting adults in the not too distant future will be able to enjoy sex over the telephone. First they will slip into undergarments lined with sensors and miniature actuators. Then they will dial their partner and, while whispering endearments, fondle each other over long-distance lines. For those who prefer something tamer, Nobel physicist Arno Penzias believes that in the 21st century it will be possible to play Ping-Pong (or any other sport) with phantasms that look and talk like the celebrity of your choice. And that's just the beginning. Someday, says visionary engineer K. Eric Drexler, molecular single-size machines will be able to assemble objects one at a time. Using this method, they could manufacture everything from prefabricated skyscrapers to computers small enough to fit inside a living cell.

When asked to close their eyes and imagine the shape of technology in the 21st century, scientists and industrial planners describe a world filled with intelligent machines, multisensual media and artificial creatures so highly evolved they will seem as alive as dogs and cats. If even their most conservative projections come true, then the next century may bring advances no less momentous than the Bomb, the Pill, and the digital computer. Should the more radical predictions prove correct, our descendants may encounter technological upheavals that could make 20th century breakthroughs seem tame.

Philip Elmer-Dewitt, "The Century Ahead: Dream Machines, Technology Watchers Foresee a World Filled with Multisensual Media, Smart Roads and Robots that are Almost Alive," *Time* (Fall 1992), p. 39.

Why would two professors of management write a book about unreality, especially one that focuses so heavily on television? Because the phenomenon of unreality is one of the most powerful illustrations of humankind's collective inability to manage technology well. Unreality falls within our purview because of our intense interest in the management of technology to the benefit of humankind.

The claims that were once made for television have virtually all been proven false. Television was to be the great educator-entertainer that would elevate the tastes and the sensibilities of the masses. Nearly no one takes this claim seriously anymore. The entertainment component of the equation so thoroughly dominates every aspect of TV and the mass media that literally everything has become reduced to slick and powerful images. We should have learned by now that no technology, however beneficial, comes without serious social consequences and costs.

If anything, the situation has gotten worse since *The Unreality Industry* was first written. We are inundated with shows that so blur the lines between reality and unreality that increasingly fewer of us either can or care to differentiate between them. Indeed, why care when illusion is preferable to a world/reality that has gotten even more difficult to manage? Besides, the so-called "reality recreation" shows are not only cheap to produce, but satisfy a public whose appetite is apparently insatiable for revelations concerning the most intimate details of the lives of others. There are no secrets anymore because of both the intrusive nature of the media and the willingness of more and more people to expose themselves to gain their fifteen minutes of fame.

If TV by itself were not enough, given that we don't know how to manage it, we now have the prospect of virtual reality. We can literally ("virtually"?) place ourselves "inside" TV. TV has become so much a part of us that we are more than willing to become part of it. What incredible creatures we humans are! We possess the brains to build powerful toys, but we lack the moral wisdom to control them.

Lest we be accused of exaggeration, consider a recent

poll by the Times-Mirror organization. Apparently, when asked, up to 50 percent of those who watch so-called "reality" or crime re-creation TV shows such as *Rescue 911* felt that they were watching the real thing *even when there was a clear statement at the bottom of the TV screen that the scene was a reenactment or re-creation of a supposedly real crime.*[1]

Fred Friendly has this to say:

"What do you mean Felix Bloch might not be guilty—I saw him do it on television." The conversation took place at the Denver airport, and it was with a top editor of a major metropolitan newspaper. My friend, the editor, had heard . . . ABC's news correspondent John McWethy report that the United States diplomat Felix S. Bloch was under FBI investigation and had had his State Department passport revoked for allegedly passing top-secret information to a Soviet KGB agent. My friend was aware that the FBI had previously refused to comment, but what this experienced senior editor saw in *ABC World News Tonight* was a videotape of "Felix Bloch" passing a briefcase to a "Soviet agent."

The videotape looked and sounded authentic; it was grainy, as hidden-camera film or tape often is. It was complete with an electronic time code, which law enforcement evidence usually carries and there were even crosshairs in the picture to make it look more like genuine surveillance. My friend and, one can assume, millions of Americans perceived the briefcase sequence as an impressive ABC news scoop. Peter Jennings, the network anchorman, introduced the report as an ABC exclusive, together with a lead-in containing one line of poetic irony: "We begin with a harsh reminder that secrecy sells." It was followed by the superimposed label "Exclusive." It was exclusive, alright. The startling dramatic pictures were a fraud; a fraud perpetuated by ABC News, using an actor who resembled Mr. Bloch. It matters little that later that night a second feed of the ABC's news report carried a superimposed disclaimer—"Simulation"—at the top of the screen. Most viewers thought they were watching smoking-gun evidence.[2]

---

[1] Thomas B. Rosensteil, "Viewers Found to Confuse TV Entertainment With News," *Los Angeles Times*, 17 August, 1989, p. 117.
[2] Fred W. Friendly, "On Television: News, Lies and Videotape," *New York Times*, Arts and Leisure Section, 6 August 1989, pp. 1, 27.

If the lines between nearly every conceivable aspect of our physical and mental environments either have become or are in the process of becoming radically blurred, then some of the major rationalizations or defenses by which the TV and other media industries have defended themselves are invalid at best. At worst, they represent outright demagoguery. Again and again one encounters six major arguments that those who work in virtually all media use to defend what they do:

1. The people themselves are largely to blame for and deserve what they get because they are inordinately and inherently stupid (the Grand Stupidity thesis).
2. We only give the people what they want.
3. If people don't like what they see or what they listen to, they can either turn off their sets or switch channels.
4. What's wrong with entertainment?
5. If we don't give the people what they want, somebody else will.
6. People can differentiate between what's "hard or real news" and what's entertainment.

It is undoubtedly true that the public itself ultimately must accept a large part of the blame for the dreadful state of American TV and culture, which could not survive, let alone prosper, if there were not a significant demand for it. However, even if the Grand Stupidity thesis were true in its entirety, this does not excuse or relieve the media from their responsibilities. What the media all too conveniently ignore in the equation is that they are fundamentally responsible not only for feeding on this "stupidity" but for encouraging it to the benefit of their huge profits. To say that the public is solely responsible for its own stupidity is to ignore the symbiotic relationship that exists between those who are supposedly stupid and those who feed and profit from it. Even more, it is to ignore the tremendous role that the media play in both creating and furthering such stupidity. It is also to ignore, by not examining it, the moral and ethical principles upon which the behavior and policies of the media rest. Just stating this major moral principle is enough to see how utterly ridiculous it is: "Whenever a segment of the public exists (and of course, the bigger the better) that is stupid enough to consume whatever we produce, then we are justified morally in satisfying that need or demand."

The second argument, "We only give the people what they want," is the argument of the drug dealer and pornographer. First of all, leaving aside its moral implications, the argument is only partly true at best. If the media were giving the people what they truly want, then why do new network shows fail at such an alarmingly high rate? The media themselves are more than willing to admit that they can't predict the taste of the public. This is precisely one of the reasons why so many movies and TV shows ape one another.

One can't have it both ways. It can't be argued that one is giving the public what they want when so much of what is presented fails spectacularly. More important is the notion that the media *only fulfill* an already existing demand, and do not, like the drug dealer, participate in the creation and maintenance of the demand. This conveniently ignores not only the symbiotic relationship that always exists between the producer and the buyer of a product or service, but also the differential power of the media themselves in creating, maintaining, and shaping needs.

No matter what field of human endeavor one investigates, one knows that "moral rock bottom" has been reached whenever a party defends what they do in terms of "We only give them what they want." If they had a better, stronger moral principle to trot out, they would surely do so in order to defend their activities. The fact that the media repeatedly fall back on such a line of reasoning in order to justify what they do shows how incredibly shaky is the moral foundation upon which they stand.

The third argument, "If people don't like what they are getting, they can always turn off their sets or switch channels," is especially interesting. This argument is symptomatic of either the outright refusal of the media to recognize the full nature of the impact they make, their inability to do so, ignorance of this impact, or all of the above. Whatever the true case, this particular argument may be the most demagogic of all.

TV has insinuated itself thoroughly throughout our culture through the general and widespread adoption of its general format and look by such newspapers as *USA Today* and magazines such as *Business Week*. It is now virtually impossible to distinguish between where TV leaves off and our general culture begins. Thus the argument that "If you don't like what you see and hear, either turn it off or switch" is truly preposterous. It refuses to recognize, let alone understand, that it's impossible to turn off a whole culture! *One can physically turn off a set, but one cannot turn off its effects if they are so deeply imbedded throughout a culture.* It may be comforting to believe that flipping a switch or turning a dial allows independence and freedom of thought and action, but such actions largely symbolic, devoid of any true significance.

> "Violence is imposing itself on producers and directors because it's cheap," [George] Gerbner [a professor in the Annenberg School of Communications at the University of Pennsylvania] said, contending that viewers cannot exercise the right to avoid "entertaining murders" and otherwise violent-laden programs.
>
> "You can change channels but you do not have a choice. We are born into it," he said. "Like the wallpaper on the wall, you absorb its [TV's] pattern without even knowing it."[3]

The third argument also conveniently ignores the fact that if everything on TV—whether on public, commercial, cable, or special access channels—increasingly looks alike, then the proliferation of the number of channels is not equivalent to an increase in the quality of choice. This argument not only confuses *quantity* of choice with *quality*, it deliberately obscures the truth that choice is merely an illusion. The sad fact is that in its constant battle to raise funding, public TV is being forced to adopt many of the

---

[3] Shawn Pogatchnik, "Kids TV Gets More Violent Study Finds: Saturday Morning Cartoons Average A Violent Act Nearly Every Other Minute, According to a Three Year Study by Annenberg School," *Los Angeles Times*, 26 January 1990, pp. F1, F27.

same techniques and formats as that of commercial TV. Proponents of this line of reasoning would have us believe that public TV can remain off by itself in some protected realm, remote from all that is taking place around us.

Finally, the third argument also ignores the fact that the odds are stacked against the individual viewer by means of the collective power that the media industry wields. The media pursue a deliberate business strategy as part of an organized industry. Against this power is arrayed the efforts of a largely unorganized, passive collection of individuals. The key notion is the deliberate business strategy of an organized industry:

> Macabre headlines ripped through the air like shots from a machine gun at the daily staff meeting of Industry R&D— a television research company that scours the back roads of the country in search of the brutal, the bizarre and, occasionally, the uplifting.
>
> The man who murdered his parents when he was 13 kills his wife and children many years later. An HIV-positive transsexual is accused of attempting to kill others through sex. A 9-year old genius is denied entrance to college. A man who raped and killed a 12-year-old girl escapes from prison. . . .
>
> Such is the stuff in which Tom Colbert, a former KCBS-TV Channel 2 news research and story department director for "Hard Copy," is building his Hollywood dream. He supplies news tips to TV's tabloid and reality shows and hopes soon to add TV-movie producers to his client list. . . .
>
> Though he can't deny that he deals mostly in the dirty laundry and tragic wreckage of once private lives, Colbert denies that he is a sleaze-merchant or ambulance chaser. He contends that he searches mostly for stories that people can learn from—stories with strong characters and messages about justice.
>
> "We have fun and do some tabloid stories that are more titillating than educational. We're always going gawk," Colbert said. But no one under 30 is reading hard news. This is where they can get their information, and if I can find stories that explore the motivations of the main character, then it is not a waste of time.[4]

---

[4] Steve Weinstein, "The Tireless Tipster to Tabloid Television," *Los Angeles Times*, 22 October 1992, pp. F1, F11.

The fourth argument, "What's wrong with entertainment?" is akin to the question "What's wrong with dessert?" The answer of course is "Nothing, except when it becomes the whole meal." A society that has become so addicted to froth and entertainment in order to function is not exactly a society that is prepared to face hard realities, let alone change—and even more, sacrifice—in order to meet them.

The fifth argument, "If we don't do it, then someone else will," is also pathetic from a moral standpoint. The moral translation of this argument is: *Whenever there exists at least one other party in the world willing to commit an evil, whether for profit or not, then one is justified, if not warranted, in committing that evil oneself; further, the sooner one beats the competition in doing it, the better.* Expressed in this form, the principle is too outrageous to warrant analysis.

The Times-Mirror study mentioned on page four is evidence of the inability of a significant percent of the population to differentiate.

At their heart, all of the six arguments and rationalizations rest on their proponents' unwillingness or inability to face the fact that we live in a world interrelated along every conceivable dimension. In earlier, simpler eras reality could be broken down into relatively stable, independent parts—much like a big machine can be decomposed into its separate, autonomous components—but this cannot be done in a world where everything is part of a highly interconnected electronic system. A system by definition is an entity with various subparts that neither have a separate existence nor function apart from the larger whole in which they exist. For instance, the human heart, lungs, or eyes neither exist nor function completely outside of the entire human body, of which they are merely parts.

To counter the previous six arguments, it is enough to consider that TV may be the "true" educational system of the United States. Surely no one can argue that TV is not one of the major reflectors, if not creators, of the value system of U.S. society.

Every evening, the New York Life Insurance Company flies all of its daily billings to Ireland. This is not primarily because wage rates are cheaper in Ireland, which indeed

they are, but because New York Life cannot find enough
trained workers to read the company's billings and process
them into a computer. Lacking the presence of a trained
work force, it is cheaper for New York Life to fly all of its
billings to Ireland than to try to correct the defects of an
untrained, uneducated work force. If this is indeed the
case, then it makes a mockery of many of the proposals
that have been put forth by American business leaders in
order to correct the ills of our educational system. It is all
right and even necessary for business leaders such as David
Kerns,[5] president of Xerox, to argue that the United States
must put its incredible resources behind teachers. We must
also become a society that truly celebrates and rewards excellence.

All of this is fine indeed, and to be applauded. However,
what this so conveniently ignores is that many of the very
businesses complaining so loudly about their inability to
find enough workers sufficiently trained to follow the complex directions needed to produce goods that can compete
in a global economy are some of the same businesses that
sponsor so much of what we see on television. If big business thinks that it can sponsor all kinds of trivial and junk
TV and then turn around and put the burden of correcting
this solely on the educational system, then it is truly more
stupid than many of us already believe.

Although we thought we had made it clear in the first
edition, *The Unreality Industry* is not primarily a diatribe
against TV. True, we focus heavily on TV, but only because it is one of the clearest arenas in which to observe
the phenomenon of unreality. Also, TV is one of our major
cultural icons.

A full-fledged study of unreality would, of course, also
treat shopping malls and theme parks, among many other
forms.[6] The fact that these two types are themselves merging, as for example in the West Edmonton Mall, the world's

---

[5] David T. Kerns and Dennis P. Doyle, *Winning the Brain Race, A Bold
Plan To Make Our Schools Competitive* (San Francisco: ICS Press), 1989.
[6] Margaret Crawford, The "Malling of America," in *Variations on a Theme
Park: Scenes from the New American City*, Michael Sorkin, ed. (New York:
Pantheon, 1990).

largest, illustrates that the phenomenon of "blurring" is rampant throughout Western culture.

The significant question is, of course, "Why is Western culture such a fertile ground for the development of unreality?" Unfortunately, there are no systematic answers to this question, only hints. For instance, Umberto Eco has pointed out that the United States has more theme parks per capita than any people on the face of the planet.[7] And Jean Beaudrillard has observed acutely that the real purpose of Disneyland is to obscure the fact that all of America is the "true" Disneyland.[8]

Western culture has become a crazy mixture of objects and images. Both, to use Beaudrillard's rich language, have "imploded" into our consciousness. The result is that we have become the very objects we consume, only now they have consumed us. And the glue that once held it all together—ideas—has been replaced by "all-consuming images."[9] Western culture has thus achieved in fact a unity of the material and the ideational worlds, but not in the ways that were once hoped for.

Finally, we also readily acknowledge that the first edition of *The Unreality Industry* did not go far enough in suggesting corrective actions. We have one suggestion that is as obviously controversial as it is difficult to implement. While all of TV needs to be radically reformulated through its *un*commercialization, we would start with TV news, if not all news, including newspapers. TV news especially should be mandated as a public service as a requirement for station licensing. The commercialization of TV news is probably one of the worst things that ever happened both to television and to American society. The commercialization of TV news has made it into a game show.

---

[7] Umberto Eco, *Travels in Hyper Reality* (New York: Harcourt, Brace, Jovanovich, 1983).

[8] Jean Beaudrillard, *America*, trans. Chris Turner (London: Verso, 1988).

[9] Stuart Ewen, *All-Consuming Images* (New York: Basic Books, 1988).

Preface

The thesis of *The Unreality Industry* is that the deliberate creation of unreality is one the most pivotal social forces shaping our time.

From our very beginning as a nation, the U.S. has been on a collision course with reality. The situation today, however, is particularly dangerous. For all practical purposes, reality has lost out. A pervading, powerful sense of unreality infiltrates the land. Unreality has become in effect our primary mode of reference. It dominates how and what we think of ourselves and others, how we define our problems and shape our actions; in short, how we define our world.

The Unreality Industry is about a disturbing phenomenon—ourselves. It is about how we have empowered TV to become one of the most powerful forces in our lives. The consequence is that TV not only defines what is reality, but much more importantly and disturbingly, TV obliterates the very distinction, the very line, between reality and unreality.

A primary contention of *The Unreality Industry* is that TV is far from being harmless. TV is both salient and dangerous at the same time. It is the primary arena for one of the most important experiments occurring in contemporary society. It is the primary testing ground for much of what we call reality. It is our central laboratory for the manufacture of unreality.

As the reality of the outside world has become increasingly complex, especially in the years since World War II, we have developed a fascination with unreality that is virtually psychopathic. The purpose of this transfiguration of common sense—our fascination with it—is to avoid coping with a complex world.

The "industry" part of unreality turns on the fact that, as a society, we no longer leave the invention of unreality to random chance or accident. No way. Unreality is big business. It involves the expenditure of billions of dollars annually. It is deliberately manufactured and sold on a gigantic scale. The end result is a society less and less able to face its true problems directly, honestly, and intelligently.

The primary contentions of *The Unreality Industry* are that TV and other vehicles of mass communication and entertainment have degraded our general level of education and debased our national discourse. Instead of grappling honestly with our problems, i.e., of dealing directly with reality itself, the inevitable drift to unreality reaches new lows.

The "promise" of TV and other instruments of mass communication has ironically been achieved; the result is not a "pretty picture." It is certainly not the one intended by the pioneers of the medium. As Paddy Chayefsky once put it, "Television is democracy at its ugliest." And as Fred Friendly once remarked, "Commercial television makes so much money doing its worst, it can't afford to do its best."

Los Angeles Times columnist Jack Smith summarized the matter as follows:

> Donald McDonald of Santa Barbara said he was reminded of Robert Hutchins' farewell address to students at

the University of Chicago in 1951, when TV was a fledgling.

"The horrid prospect," Hutchins said, "that television opens before us, with nobody speaking and nobody reading, suggests that a bleak and torpid epic may lie ahead which, if it lasts long enough, will gradually, according to the principles of evolution, produce a population indistinguishable from the lower forms of plant life.

"Astronomers at the University of Chicago have detected something that looks like moss growing on Mars. I am convinced that Mars was once inhabited by rational human beings like ourselves, who had the misfortune, some thousands of years ago, to invent television."*

Unreality is a complex, multifaceted phenomenon. As a result, in this book we take a hard look at its various aspects in a systematic manner. We argue, among other things, that unreality results from:

(a) The ways in which the human mind is structured; i.e., a fundamental part of unreality arises from the ways in which our minds are organized;
(b) Our unique cultural history that predisposes the U.S. especially towards a cult of unreality;
(c) The vast, powerful entertainment industry and the influence it now wields over every part of U.S. society;
(d) The characteristics of the various communication media themselves, e.g., TV.

To our knowledge, this is the only book that explicitly contrasts side by side:

(a) The characteristics of the new reality that has arisen since World War II, i.e., a world of vast complexity and global interdependence, and
(b) The deliberate, systematic manufacturing of unreality that has emerged primarily in reaction to our

---

*Jack Smith, "Seeing Eye to Eye With More Couch Potatoes," *Los Angeles Times*, September 14, 1988, Part V, p. 1.

inability to cope with this new world of perverse complexity.

One of the primary aims of *The Unreality Industry* is to show the opposition and the tension that exist between the forces that compose the "new global reality" and those which give rise to the "new unrealities." The contrast can be easily summarized:

Characteristics of the New Global Reality	*Characteristics of the New Unreality*
1. Increased, if not overwhelming, complexity through longer and longer trains of thought necessary to achieve a proper understanding of any event or phenomenon of modern society.	1. Greater and greater simplified, if not trivialized, versions of everything through the presentation of vast amounts of uncorrelated data, quick-moving and unrelated images, so that not only is there no need to connect them, but that it literally defies the ability of anyone to connect them in a coherent pattern.
2. More and more spheres of life that are thrown together into instant and strange conjunctions than ever before.	2. More and more 15- to 20-second snips or sound bites of limited and simplified contextless information which concentrate mainly on a single point of view through the use of one liners, and countless disconnected images.
3. The quickened pace of all events through the ability to communicate rapidly through computers; increased general stress in our lives.	3. The focus on short term goals such as money, notoriety, instant fame, the attempt to create stability by refusing to update our views of the world.
4. Socially, economically and morally we are soon becoming if we have not already become a second-rate nation.	4. We continue to believe that we are the biggest and the best.
5. More and more our destiny is controlled by other nations.	5. We continue to believe we can get along just fine without others.
6. More and more our values are severely in question.	6. We continue to believe that we are God's chosen people, that our moral destiny is to shape the world.

Make no mistake. This book is not about TV, or TV bashing. TV is simply a convenient metaphor that provides one of the clearest arenas in which to observe the operation and development of unreality.

The major defect of most treatments of TV and other aspects of contemporary culture is that they are largely conducted in isolation from many of the other major forces that are occurring simultaneously in modern societies. In the Systems Age, no major force or aspect of society can be looked at or studied in isolation—or ignored.* To do so is to miss many of the most essential properties of the phenomena being studied. In the Systems Age, nothing either exists or can be understood in isolation. Thus, one of the most essential, distinctive characteristics of *The Unreality Industry* is that the phenomenon of unreality itself is seen as a characteristic feature of the Systems Age. As a result, the phenomenon of unreality manifests itself on several different levels of society simultaneously.

Of course, the final, burning question is: "Can anything be done about our society's obsession with unreality, and correspondingly our flight from reality?" We're not certain. But, we do suggest several courses of action. In the end, however, the best solution may be that which comes out of moral outrage, and not a "scholarly, objective, disinterested" examination of the matter. If in the end we have contributed to an *informed, moral outrage*, then we will have achieved one of our primary aims.

---

*See Russell L. Ackoff, *Creating the Corporate Future, Plan or Be Planned For*, New York, John Wiley, 1981; C. West Churchman, *Thought and Wisdom*, Seaside, CA, Intersystems Publications, 1982; and Ian I. Mitroff, *Break-Away Thinking, How to Challenge Your Business Assumptions (And Why You Should)*, New York, John Wiley, 1988, for a discussion of the transition from the Machine Age to the Systems Age and the respective characteristics and differences between both ages.

The Unreality
Industry

1. The Age of Unreality
The Entertainment Society

...Why did attorneys for Malibu home owners choose TV's *People's Court* Judge Joseph A. Wapner to disburse up to $75 million won by the homeowners in a suit against the California Department of Transportation?

Wapner's twenty years on the Superior Court bench before he retired in 1979 helped. So did the fact that last year he handled the disbursement of $8.75 million to 120 families in a Fullerton suit.

But equally as important was Wapner's six years of television exposure, according to the attorneys involved, who believe his visibility built a large audience among the plaintiffs in the case.

"He starts with credibility and that is very important to these people's confidence, that they're going to be treated fairly...."

But where do you draw the line between television and reality?

"I think when someone steps out of reality into television, they ought to stay there and not journey back and forth willy-nilly," said Tom Shales, television critic of the *Wash-*

ington Post. "We have enough problems separating reality and fantasy thanks to television.... It leads to confusion and disorientation among viewers."

—Gary Libman, "'People's Court' Judge Wapner Sparks $75 Million Debate," *Los Angeles Times,* Aug. 6, 1987, Part IV, p. 1.

The world, we are told, has always been complex. If we could go back in time and talk directly to the people of any era, chances are they would say, "The complexity of our world far outstrips anything that people before us had to face." For most people, the lesson to be drawn is that "nothing is really new; people have always felt that their age is the pinnacle of complexity." So put, the lesson is really a thinly veiled command to "Shut up! Stop complaining!"

And yet, there is something in us that won't be shut up. Even if every generation before us has felt the same, the feeling that there is something truly different about our times will not go away.

Something *is* different. The size, the scope, the magnitude of our problems, our existence, is different. Our existence and our problems are so interconnected, so intertwined, that no one knows where to begin in stating them let alone in solving them.

An example: Recently CBS Evening News ran a segment on the global nature of the drug problem particularly as it affects the U.S. With all the money that the U.S. currently spends on drug enforcement, U.S. officials are only able to seize on the average ten percent of the drugs entering the country. And this is the result of our having thrown vast sums of money at the problem over many years and doing most of the things that have been recommended by various law enforcement and government agencies. What is particularly disheartening is that even if the U.S. were to increase substantially its efforts, it might stop only an additional ten percent. And stopping an additional ten percent would only make the problem get worse, not better! It would drive up the price of the remaining 80 percent, thus only increasing further the wealth of the

Colombian drug lords. It would not stop appreciably the flow of drugs into the U.S. and the resulting problems. Indeed, U.S. drug addicts would have to steal even more in order to pay the higher price of drugs. *The* solution? *A* solution, if there is one?

A parade of conservatives and liberals, including former police officials who are quick to point out that they are not "bleeding hearts," recommended legalizing drugs, thus undercutting the economics of the whole process. After having tried so many other solutions over the years, no other one seems possible. However much sense this solution might make, it only raises other problems such as, is it politically feasible? Is it morally acceptable?

And so we have the basis of a deeper problem. The drug problem can only be "solved" by a "solution" that is as radical or horrendous as the initial problem itself. However, the solution, legalizing drugs, is topsy turvy. It goes deeply against the grain of the original intention, which is to lower drastically the use of drugs in our society. And yet here is a potential solution that argues in effect that to remove the problem you have to make the source of drugs more freely available.

The point of the example is not whether one agrees fully with the particular solution. The point is that so many of our current problems seem to generate the same general kind of solution. The solution consists of intensifying the initial problem itself! In the case of drugs, one lowers the high crime rate connected with the purchase of drugs by increasing the supply of low cost drugs. One solves the original problem, as it were, at the "expense" of creating another problem.

Another example: New technology potentially creates as many new problems as it solves. While no one knows for sure how much, technology was thought to be a major factor in the October 1987 crash of the stock market. Through the use of computers and extensive electronic networks, the whole financial structure of the planet is completely interconnected. Literally billions of dollars flow around the globe daily at the stroke of keys pressed on computers. The result is that *there is only one stock market worldwide*. Tokyo, New York, and London are only branches of this one interconnected global market. One of the consequences is that if there is deep panic in one branch of the market, for example New York, then it is only, literally, a short matter of time before the panic spreads around the globe to all branches. The only factor preventing the panic from acting instantaneously is that the various branches close down at night, i.e., wherever night happens to be on the face of the planet. The computers and networks, however, are "on" all the time. The end result is a new phenomenon—*global stock market panic.*

As long as people invest and there are huge sums of money to be made and lost, there will always be greed and panic. What's different is that today's greed and panic operate at lightning speed. Greed and panic are exacerbated by computers and electronic networks operating at the speed of light. The result is that we have beings with essentially the same emotional makeup as they had in the fifth century operating 21st century systems of vast complexity such that no one can say for sure how they or we will behave.

A final example: Technology not only creates new problems but new "diseases" as well. Computers have given rise to a whole new kind of disease called computer viruses. These are not viruses in the strict biological sense but are instead computer programs that invade and attack the logic of the host computers into which they are input. Many of the viruses are so sophisticated that they cannot be detected by the most sophisticated of means. Indeed the viruses are often concealed within so-called normal or friendly-appearing programs that are used to run computer systems. What's more, they are often embedded within modern day Trojan Horses, i.e., inside free gifts that are sent to the operators of computer systems.

What's interesting is that increasingly, like every other problem in modern society, the problem of computer viruses has a global dimension. Computer viruses have already attacked the computer systems of large, multinational corporations like IBM. The result is that once-sacred geopolitical borders are increasingly irrelevant. The real fear is that computer viruses will invade the programs of unparalleled size and complexity that are needed to run Star Wars, thus dooming the whole effort.

Whether the world has always appeared complex to man is really beside the point. It is becoming clear that as reality itself has become increasingly complex over the course of this century in particular, the ability of the average citizen to make sense of that complexity has diminished accordingly. Worse yet, our interest in making sense of reality has declined in direct proportion to our inability to make sense of it.

It has also become clear that when the world can no longer be made coherent, either through explanation or action, then we seek coherence elsewhere. In a world gone mad as the result of overwhelming complexity, the need for coherence does not diminish. Its need becomes even greater. If we cannot find coherence in ideas or intellectual patterns alone, then we seek it in alternate forms, e.g., in a cult of personalities; in pseudo pop heroes; in entertaining and amusing faces that soothe over our need for satisfying explanations. If the latter part of the 20th century has succeeded in anything, it is in the deliberate manufacturing and distribution of celebrities on a wide scale. We have developed a fascination with celebrities that borders on the sociopathic.

The fascination with celebrities, however, is only part of a larger, virtually unexplored phenomenon. In recent years, it has become fashionable to engage in culture bashing of various forms: celebrities (Schickel[1]), TV (Postman[2] and Meyerowitz[3]), and education (Bloom[4]). While there is much in the theses of all of these critics with which we agree, we believe that each of them has only been scratching the surface of a much larger phenomenon. It is this larger phenomenon which is the unifying force underlying their separate criticisms. As a result, however insightful their separate criticisms may be, they miss something essential because of their failure to see the underlying general phenomenon which is at work. This general phenomenon is unreality.

The main message of *The Unreality Industry* is that the

U.S. is on a collision course with reality. As the outside world became increasingly complex, especially in the intervening years since World War II, so that no one person or institution could fully understand or control it, we not only lost interest in dealing with reality per se but we invented substitute realities. Somehow, we became more adept at dealing with these substitute realities, or unrealities as we call them. Indeed, unreality itself has become a major growth industry. Its forms and varieties have proliferated continually over the course of the 20th century.

The fundamental purpose of all forms of unreality is to provide an illusion of control. If men cannot control the realities with which they are faced, then they will invent unrealities over which they can maintain the illusion of control.

The "industry" part of unreality concerns the fact that as a society, we no longer leave the invention of unreality to random chance or accident. Unreality is big business. It is manufactured and sold on a gigantic scale. It has intruded itself into every aspect of our lives. For example, by some estimates, public relations, i.e., the deliberate manufacturing of slanted information, accounts for up to 70 percent of what passes for news and information in our society.[5] The end consequence is a society less and less able to face its true problems directly, honestly, and intelligently. A further consequence is that it takes crises of increasing impact, for example the recent crash of the stock market, to redirect our attention back to reality, if then. However, even mega-crises may no longer be sufficient to capture our attention in a society that has become anesthetized to crises of all kinds. As the *Wall Street Journal* has noted:

> How does one separate illusion from reality in an electronic society that serves up visions of disaster nearly every day? It could be that most Americans experienced the [stock market] crash as yet another media event, something witnessed but not quite real. "People are getting used to the idea of sudden media traumas followed by sudden media recoveries," says Todd Domke, a Boston-area political consultant. "Great public crises come and go—Gary Hart, the Persian Gulf, airplane crashes—but life goes on. People are accepting this weird way of life as a given."[6]

This book is a systematic examination of the definition and various meanings of unreality, the various means by which it is produced, its impacts on individuals, and our society as a whole. The phenomenon of unreality can not be understood by examining any single facet or level of society. The phenomenon is so multifaceted that it defies both definition and examination through any single lens. Indeed, to try to focus on one aspect to the exclusion of others is to miss one of the most essential qualities of unreality. One of the reasons why unreality is so powerful a force in our society is precisely that it is the result of a combination of mutually reinforcing influences. Thus, this is not a book which is an in-depth treatment of unreality in such separate fields as TV, newspapers, religion, film, politics, etc., although we use abundant examples from each of them to illustrate the general nature of unreality. This is a book about the *general phenomenon* of unreality because it is the general phenomenon which is the unifying force influencing much of which goes on in American life today.

The Unreality Industry not only examines the role that the various communication media (e.g., TV, newspapers) play in the dissemination and fostering of unreality, but it also shows that the role of the various communication media can not be properly understood unless we also understand how they function within the even larger entertainment industry. In a similar fashion, we can not understand how the larger entertainment industry fosters and shapes our receptivity to unreality unless we also understand how the broader fabric of American culture and values and our unique history have shaped our special cultural disposition towards unreality.

For all practical purposes, the U.S. today is a 24-hour, TV entertainment society. Everything in contemporary America is an entertainment, from sporting event to big business, politics, certainly religion, and even academia. If it isn't fun, cute, or packaged in a ten-second sound bite, then forget it. If it can't be presented with a smiling, cheerful, sexy face, then it ain't worth attending to. We're all spectators in a grand entertainment society looking up at the few superstars on the stage who not only perform but stand out enough to be labeled heroes of our age. In critic Richard Schickel's biting observation, in contemporary America one is either a celebrity or one is nothing.

America is thus indeed on a collision course with reality: the denial of complexity continues to reach new lows. One need only mention Gary Hart, Ronald Reagan, Oral Roberts, Jim and Tammy Bakker, and of course the latest in the series, Jimmy Swaggert, to show that the denial of reality has now become one of our principal art forms. For example, as he abruptly left the presidential race the first time around, Gary Hart suggested that he was simply too good for us. Defrocked TV minister Jim Bakker insisted he had an affair with his secretary in order to save his marriage. And Ronald Reagan, having said initially that he knew nothing about the gun runs to the Contras, later said that not only did he know about it, but that it was his idea. Oral Roberts, Bakker's fellow TV minister, went up in a tower and said that God would strike him dead if people didn't send him lots of money right away. Rather than protesting all this doubletalk and doublethink, the American people seem not only to accept it but to understand it. After all, how is one to differentiate between Jimmy Swaggert's confession of sin on TV and his normal act? The cycle of sin, denial, confession, and sin again is thus another of our principal forms of entertainment. To complete the circle, entertainment itself is one of the biggest factors contributing to the denial of reality, and hence, to the continued rise of unreality. This, then, is the Age of Unreality and Disinformation.

One of the other central messages of *The Unreality Industry* is that it has become increasingly difficult to say what is real any longer. The general predisposition towards the increased use of entertainment as a substitute for dealing directly with our problems, especially as entertainment has been aided by modern technology,[7] has blurred the fine line at best between reality and unreality. We have become so adept at the manufacturing and consumption of fantasy that the distinction between reality and unreality is now virtually meaningless. If anything, unreality is the new reality. While this state of affairs can by no means be solely attributed to the White House, Ronald Reagan, when he was president, did not help. When a persistent and repeated disdain for the facts emanates from the highest office of the land,[8] when personal fantasy is repeatedly substituted for reality,[9] then the result is the further seepage of unreality into American life.

To be sure, reality and complexity are themselves complex and hence not easily defined. Nevertheless, the main features of unreality have become clear enough so that we can discern two major forms. It should be noted that it is much easier to define each type in theory than it is to keep them apart in practice.

The first major form of unreality, or what we shall call Unreality One, is very close to what has been called Artificial Reality.[10] *Unreality One refers to the fact that we are now so close to creating electronic images of any existing or imaginary person, place, or thing that an electronic image and a real person can interact at the same time on a computer screen or TV so that a viewer cannot tell whether one or both of the images are real or not.* Thus, for instance, in the foreseeable future, it is within possibility to project an image of President Bush and General Secretary Gorbachev shaking hands or hitting one another so that one will not be able to tell whether the scene projected is "real" or doctored.[11]

Consider another example. If we think that there have been howls of protest accompanying the colorization of black and white movie classics, then it will be nothing compared to what's already in the works. When we are able to store electronically an image of, say, Jane Fonda in a computer, then what is there to prevent the Fonda image from being substituted for that of Meryl Streep in *Out of Africa* so that if one wanted to see Fonda in the role, one could do it without having to reshoot the entire movie? What do movie stars do in this not implausible scenario? Do they sell or copyright their electronic images outright? But why not, in a society where celebrities are more than willing to sell every fragment of their being or personality for profit?

All this pertains to Unreality One.

Unreality Two is akin to Pseudo Reality. *It is the deliberate denial and distortion of reality, i.e., complexity, through the massive infusion of entertainment into every aspect of society which on its surface purports to deal with reality.* One of the most important illustrative examples of this phenomenon is TV news, with which we will deal shortly. News which is supposed to give us information in order to function more effectively in a complex world can be seen to perpetuate Unreality Two.

Although there are important overlaps between these two forms of unreality, there are important critical differences nonetheless. Unreality One or Artificial Reality makes the unreal look so real that we cannot tell the difference between the two. Unreality Two or Pseudo Reality, on the other hand, makes the unreal so entertaining that we no longer care about reality. Under Unreality One we can no longer differentiate between reality and unreality even if we wanted to. Under Unreality Two *we no longer care to differentiate* between reality and unreality even if we could.

In order to gain a feel for the whole phenomenon of unreality, let us turn briefly to an examination of TV news.

An Introduction to Pseudo Reality: TV News as Entertainment[12]

Few critical observers, including the networks themselves, resist any longer the notion that TV news has become so infused by the techniques of entertainment that for all practical purposes TV news has become just another form of entertainment. The morning news shows have so consciously and deliberately adopted entertainment formats that the networks not only admit openly that they have become pure entertainment, but they even discuss and debate the percentages of entertainment content versus news content the shows are supposed to have. It's probably even fairer to say that at best the thinking of the news networks is perfectly schizophrenic on the issue:

CBS Entertainment President Kim Le Masters raised some eyebrows the other day when he told visiting TV critics that his network had taken steps in "breaking down the corroded barriers" between the entertainment and news divisions.

But CBS News President Howard Stringer and "CBS Evening News" anchor Dan Rather insist that, although CBS has made progress recently in getting news programming considered for prime time, the line between reporting and entertainment is in no danger of being blurred at CBS.[13]

Having crossed over the line into entertainment, the nightly news programs not only face competition from other news programs which are also trying to jockey their position but from other prime time TV programs they are trying to displace.[14]

That TV news has become almost pure entertainment is clear from its adoption of most of the techniques that are characteristic of entertainment. The most obvious, familiar, and easily seen characteristics are its surface features:

1. The glitzy, hi-tech studio sets;

2. the pretty faces and pleasing, entertaining personalities of the anchors and special assignment people;

3. the easy flowing conversation and back and forth banter among the news team that has the appearance of being spontaneous but is often rehearsed as much as any talk show (at best we witness a form of improvisational melodrama);

4. the fact that rarely if ever do we witness open conflict, debate, and confrontation between the news anchors;

5. the fact that mainly only surface issues in the form of numbers get reported (e.g., how many mines there are in the Persian Gulf, how many enemy soldiers have been captured, etc.), not the deeper why's of a situation;

6. the stunning visuals which generally introduce the shows by zooming in on the city or region in relation to the rest of the U.S.;

7. the slick graphics that transition the movement between news segments;

8. the tantalizing teasers with their accompanying provocative headlines announcing segments to come;

9. the intermingling of the titillating and the humorous with the semi-serious, especially on the morning "news" programs;

10. the constant interspersing of the bizarre, celebrity guest-spots, the inane, and the potentially world shattering.

The overall effect is one where the studio set, the look and the feel of the show, the newscasters as both personal friends and storytellers of a very special kind to the viewing public predominate.

(TV is not the only medium alone in adopting these techniques. For instance, a Los Angeles morning radio show regularly presents the day's headlines in the form of singing news commercials. For another, *Business Week* advertises in competition with *Fortune* and the *Wall Street Journal* on TV—where else?—that "We don't just inform you but we entertain you." [Is *Business Week* really serious? Are we to expect the following: "Ha Ha Ha, Ha! The stock market just crashed! What a laugh! The U.S. has just been taken over by the Germans and the Japanese! Your company is about to go down the tubes! What fun!] The covers of *Business Week* themselves flashing by on the screen are virtually indistinguishable from the best of TV graphics. The message is that busy executives don't have time to read in depth so don't waste your time reading the *Wall Street Journal* every day when one quick bite of *Business Week* once a week is sufficient to give you a step ahead of the competition. The 15-second read thus is to magazines what the 15-second-look bite is to TV.)

One of the most generally distinctive features of TV has been noted by a number of distinguished analysts;[15] it bears repeating in the context of TV news for it allows us to interpret it in a way that has not been done before. Television news, like all TV, presents itself in a grossly simplified, if not distorted, way. All issues are stripped down to a few catchword phrases and simplifying sentences in order to cram as many sound bites into a half-hour news segment thus giving more time for packing in commercials around them. But this means that with very few exceptions, most issues on network television news are presented in a completely ahistorical context of no context whatsoever. Most news issues, especially local items, merely appear; they drop in from out of the blue. They don't just come at the viewer, but they literally explode at the viewer off the screen. The overall effect is one of dazzling confusion. Little or no attempt is made to present a larger view in which the issues could be located in some coherent framework, for TV long ago "discovered" (whether it "discovered" or "invented" them is a matter of no small consequence) three important social facts: one, no coherent framework exists in a complex world that can make sense of everything; two, even if it did, the average viewer is not interested in it anyway; and three, even if they were interested, it would take too much dull, boring, and stressful lectures to teach it to them anyway. (As an aside, we disagree with all three of these propositions. As we argue in a later chapter, there may well be *no single pattern* or framework into which events can be neatly fitted as they could in simpler times, but it is possible to comprehend why the world has become more complex. More than we would have thought, it is possible to explain the sources of the new complexity. This understanding is itself a hopeful beginning in our coping with reality.)

In this rampant context of no context, if not deliberately orchestrated confusion, the only constant is the personalities of the TV news anchors and reporters. Many of us see them more often, certainly in our homes, than we do our friends, neighbors, relatives, and even our co-workers from whom we are increasingly distanced on our jobs anyway. As a recent Harris poll[16] points out, many of us are so stressed out on our jobs, we don't want to invite into our homes on a regular basis anyone who would perturb, anger, or raise unpleasant issues in any way. God forbid that we would actually have to engage in serious conversation which would probably lead to disagreements with which we would have to deal. Thus, a prime requisite for being a TV news anchor is not necessarily that of being on top of the news but of being able to mollify us, to soothe us after a long hard day of stress.

When ideas and events themselves no longer carry any badge or mark of instant coherency and credibility, then the cohesion we need to make sense of our lives has to be carried by some other elements in our society. In this age of huge, bureaucratic institutions, lacking not only the personal touch, care, and concern, but also regard for the dignity of either their employees or those whom they pretend to serve, what better supplier of continuity could there be than the pleasant faces who make pablum out of chaos and soothe our fragile egos by masquerading as our "friends."

One of the most consistently shrewd and penetrating observers of TV is the *Los Angeles Times'* Pulitzer Prize winning journalist Howard Rosenberg. In a column,[17] Rosenberg focused his usual acute perceptiveness on a series of promos in which KCBS, Los Angeles' local CBS affiliate, showcased its news personalities. In a highly clever and skillfully crafted series of short spots, we got to "know" the personalities through intimate mini-portraits spotlighting their lives, their interests, backgrounds, and families. The general theme is one of "we're family; you can trust us because we're just like you; we like baseball, kids, families, ect."

One of the most interesting spots featured Steve Kmetko, KCBS's entertainment editor. In the spot, we see him in his apartment, lounging casually and completely at ease in front of the camera. He recounts that he always wanted to go into show biz but he couldn't sing, dance, or act. Rosenberg zeroes in on the contradiction like a bee going straight for honey. The whole spot is so obviously well done that it had to be carefully scripted. In saying that he can't act with such sincerity Kmetko is showing what a superb actor he is, delivering his lines with the natural ease and grace of a polished performer. The whole series of spots is thus a very clever, well disguised lie. But more than this, TV news now demonstrates something deeper.

TV news is not only infused through and through with deception but with entertainment as well. Now so thoroughly a part of TV news, entertainment not only constitutes a significant portion of the content *within* the news, but it has become integral to the "content *leading up to* the news." The personalities that constitute the news not only perform on and within it, but they perform off of it as well. Anyone who appears constantly on the screen is by definition a celebrity. And to be a celebrity is to constantly fester the public's incessant need to know what the people are like who appear before them continuously. If reality doesn't satisfy that perceived public need, then unreality has to be invented in order to fill it.

There is a special term in philosophy that is particularly relevant in the context of the present discussion. It is the notion of a "guarantor."[18] Some of the most important and profound debates in philosophy center around what is a valid guarantor since so much hinges on it. The guarantor is that highly special feature of every philosophical system whose central, highly critical function is literally to "guarantee" that the system will produce what it purports to deliver. That is, truth about the natural and social worlds so that men can act accordingly to improve their lives. A great deal of the centuries-old debates between the rationalists and the empiricists center around what is a valid guarantor for producing true knowledge. For the rationalists, the preferred guarantor notions have been, among many, the logical consistency between a set of propositions that can either be derived from some initial ideas whose truth is either self-evident, presumed, taken as provisionally true, or whose opposites confound reasonableness and hence are taken to be false. For the empiricists, the preferred guarantor notions are based generally on the agreement between different qualified observers who can in principle observe the same "hard facts."

What's so fascinating about TV news is that the guarantor behind its believability—its "truths" loosely defined—is that of pleasing personalities in particular and entertainment in general.[19] As a result, there is an incredible paradox inherent in TV's guarantor notion.

TV is the direct result of a scientific, hi-tech culture. Almost all of the guarantor notions of science that have been proposed down through the ages have been based on anything but the personalities of scientists.[20] The truths of science are supposed to be objective, timeless, and universal. They are supposed to hold for all competent observers in the universe no matter what their individual personality or the culture in which they live. Scientific truths, in other words, are supposed to be judged solely on their own merits, not on those of the characteristics or attributes of their discoverers, and in the extreme, are even supposed to be independent of people. They are ideally to be characteristics of physical reality itself untouched by human hands and minds.

The paradox is that the more science has developed, the more good things it has given us, the more the general populace has retreated to non, pre-scientific modes of explanation and guarantor notions. The dream of science has always been to replace explanations of the world that are based on individual, personal experiences or particular authorities (e.g., shamans, religious authorities) with explanations that are grounded (i.e., guaranteed) by objective, impersonal mechanisms such as logical, scientific theories.

To state it again, the more that science has delivered inventions that in themselves are not only beyond the pale of most people's comprehension, but also with such abundance and speed that they literally challenge the ability of most people to make sense of them, the more people have been forced to retreat to pre-scientific guarantors to make sense of their world. The end result is that no one takes seriously any longer one of the profoundest dreams of the Enlightenment, i.e., the notion that science would liberate men generally, so that if the masses were not fluent in the detailed understanding of science or scientific method, they would at least appreciate the necessity for governing human affairs based upon the strong guidance of science.

Instead of the widespread diffusion and respect for science among the general populace, quite the reverse has occurred. The writer Robert Ashhina has noted that what we have instead is the diffusion of "social science fiction" as evidenced by the recent popularity of such books as Shere

Hite's *Women in Love,* Collette Doyling's, *The Cinderella Complex,* Dan Kiley's *Peter Pan Syndrome,* and Nancy Friday's *Men in Love.* As Carol Tavris observes: "These books consist largely of anonymous letters or interviews, but the impression that they are based on 'research' adds a veneer of respectability and seriousness, and supposedly elevates them above the authors' personal experiences."[21] The point is that our obsession with unreality is to be found increasingly throughout all of society. TV is not alone in perpetuating it.

Again, TV news is only the most explicit model for this sort of thing, so delicious that it is being adopted widely and improved on in ways that prove that modeling is the sincerest form of flattery. *USA Today,* for example, is regarded as the quintessential example of a paper explicitly designed with a TV format. *Washington Post* magazine writer David Remnick, writing in *Esquire,* put it thusly:

> ...In [*USA Today* publisher Al Neuharth's] columns and in the paper's countless graphs, lists, and "brights," *facts are popcorn, neither offensive nor nourishing. They just are* [italics ours].
>
> There are a few major newspapers in the world that show such unyielding optimism, and such an overwhelming desire to please and unite the citizenry, such an obdurate unwillingness to face the sorrows and complexities of the modern world. Most prominent among them are *Pravda* and *Izvestia.* But compared with *USA Today,* Soviet newspapers face an identity crisis. At least for now, a careful reader of *Pravda* will find stark descriptions of alcoholism, drug addiction, even sentiment against the war in Afghanistan to offset articles about heroic sugar-beet production in Murmansk.[22]

The supreme irony about TV news is that in the end it fails miserably on two accounts. First, it is not truly informative and therefore it is not really news. Second, it is not even good entertainment. If it is judged by the standard of entertainment, then it suffers seriously by comparison with what passes for real entertainment in contemporary America. It doesn't even begin to approach the true Rambo-like qualities that are now rampant throughout the rest of the entertainment industry.

If current trends continue, why shouldn't news take on the form of a game show? As we shall see in a later chapter, TV justice has already assumed precisely this form on *The People's Court.* Once traditional boundaries are no longer sacred and therefore are up for constant experimentation, and even more for commercial exploitation, no proposal, no speculation, on the future of America is too outrageous to be dismissed. To the contrary, in order to capture the current drift of where America is headed, the only valid predictor (guarantor) of America's future may be outrageousness.

A Postscript: The McBraining of the American Mind

CBS News raised a critical eyebrow or two by its 1988 decision to develop a prime time TV "news" program that would be a direct spinoff of the "newspaper" *USA Today.*[23] The concern centers around the fact that, as we have noted, *USA Today* (which subsequently became a syndicated "entertainment package" sold to local stations including those owned and operated by CBS) is itself nothing but a "newspaper version" of TV. That is, *USA Today* is a bastardized version of TV. Thus, through TV's copying of *USA Today*, the circle is not only complete but the bastardization has been taken one step further.

USA Today incorporates nearly all of TV's prominent features as a distinctive medium of communication: its articles are deliberately short, reflecting TV's incessant reduction of all ideas, trivial or serious, to 15-20 second segments; its pace, feel, and look are fast paced so as not to bore the reader and also to keep their interest through constant stimulation; abundant use is made of color and charts for the purpose of not merely simplifying important issues but more significantly for stimulating the eyes of viewers if not their brains; all ideas are by and large trivialized. *USA Today* not only makes no bones about the fact that the paper and its TV "spinoff" are modeled along the lines of pure entertainment, but it even exalts in the fact; entertainment is thus the dominant rationale for the basic appeal of both the paper and the television show as well as the basic reasons for their existence.

None of this should be really surprising once one understands that all human institutions and games operate by a distinct set of rules. Consider some of the following unwritten rules of TV. The more the medium operates, the more clearly we can see the hidden rules that make it run:

> Rule #1: Everything on TV is a deliberate staged simulation (a fake?) of a prior reality.

> What we see on TV is not "the real thing" per se but an acted, staged version of it. For instance, TV wrestling is a staged entertainment, an acted out version of real wrestling. "Wrestlers" like Hulk Hogan and Andre the Giant are really skilled, highly paid entertainers.

> Rule #2: Every simulation is capable of simulating every other simulation as well as being simulated by them.

> Rule #3: The greater the number of cycles of simulation, i.e., the number of simulations a simulation simulates, the better it is.

> Rule #4: Each cycle of simulation decreases the reality of the original thing being simulated; conversely, each cycle increases the amount of unreality.

USA Today is a perfect illustration of every one of these rules. The paper is a simulation of TV news which in turn is itself a simulation of "real news"; and the TV version bearing the name became a simulation of *USA Today*. So the circle is now complete. Each cycle of the simulation decreases our relation to the original thing, i.e., news as information, and increases the level of unreality, i.e., news as entertainment. It's like living in a closed environment where the waste products of each cycle become the intake elements to the next. We have become in other words a Garbage In and Out and In Again Society.

(None of the prior points are necessarily invalidated by the fact that at the time of our writing the TV version of *USA Today* has failed. Only the particular production has failed, not the basic concept. There were no great howls of protest and outrage towards the basic idea. Indeed, if anything, tabloid TV shows continue to grow.)

Is it any wonder then why young adults applying to college now send in videos of themselves to admissions committees? After all, if it's good enough for presidential candidates, why not also for young people? Presidential candidates now make videos of themselves so that if they can't travel up and down a state, then their videos can. And having become so used to all this, is it really strange to find that more people now prefer to watch the videos than see the real thing? Haven't we become so used to seeing videos of products in stores that even when the product is next to a TV itself, many of us prefer to watch TV? After all, if entertainment is now the norm throughout all of our society, then acting dominates over content. But if so, why shouldn't youngsters then follow the lead of our current presidents where apparently looking and sounding good are more important than ability or content—or even the character to govern?

Closing Thoughts

How did all of this come about? What can the fate of any society be that has to function in a complex world if its fundamental reason for being has degenerated into the production and comsumption of limitless amounts of unreality?

Of course, reality has never been our strong suit. "Oh beautiful, for spacious skies, for amber waves of grain, for purple mountain majesty above the fruited plain..." By 1893, when Katherine Lee Bates wrote *America the Beautiful*, once pastoral America had become a vast blast furnace and more Americans sang about spacious skies, amber waves of grain, and fruited plains than ever saw them, but, never mind. They were out there somewhere, and, if we got rich enough or brave enough, we could go and see them for ourselves.

But if we were vague and dreamy in 1893, today we are only semiconscious beings living in an imaginary land-scape. In Thoreau's phrase, *we have become the tools of our tools*. We invented a whole range of amazing machines, and now they are reinventing us. Ironically, the more sophisticated they have become, the more primitive we have become; the more active they are, the more passive we are, and the real world recedes more and more.

The U.S. is indeed on a collision course with reality. And reality may be losing if it has not done so already.

2. Beyond Our Control
Reality Run Amok

The only coherence possible today may be the understanding of why the old coherence has broken down on
every front of our existence:

> The world Machine is coming anyway, with or without
> the Media Lab. Earth is already wholly integrated. The
> coins in your pocket know about the price of oil, about
> apartheid in South Africa, about the Pope's opinions on
> birth control, about the Soviet space program, about dollar/
> yen exchange rates. All that will advance now is the rate of
> knowing, the structure of the new immediacies.
> We can anticipate calamities of the emerging, acceler-
> ating world information systems—sabotage, financial
> crashes, cultural pillagings, [false] news stories, enter-
> taining dictators. We must hope that such information
> disasters occur early and often, so that caution is built into
> us and into the systems.

—Stewart Brand, *The Media Lab*, p. 228.

...on January 27th (1988), a *test message* [italics ours] was sent out from the International Atomic Energy Agency in Vienna to weather centers in 25 countries. The message was partially coded and was transmitted on the World Meteorological Association's global telex and communications network. Clearly marked as a *test* [italics ours], it referred to a buildup of radiation over the Soviet Bloc. A few days later, the stock markets in Tokyo and Hong Kong shuttered amid sudden rumors of another Chernobyl. In a matter of hours, the fallout spread to the markets in the Middle East, Europe, and finally Wall Street. By that time, an early warning monitoring station in Sweden had been put on full alert.

—Paul Tate, "Risk! The Third Factor," *Datamation*, April 15, 1988, p. 59.

What is the reality from which we are fleeing? What is it about current reality that makes it more comforting psychologically to attempt to remake it than to deal directly with it?

Reality and unreality have always been opposite sides of the same coin. Each is a reflection, a product of, and a reaction to the other. The purpose of the first chapter was to give the reader a feel for the general phenomenon of unreality. The purpose of this chapter is to examine in depth what the nature of the new reality is and why it is so bewildering that we find it easier to flee from it than to deal with it.

There are three principal features that characterize the new reality.

1. The Failure of Success, or, The-World-Changed-Drastically-But-We-Didn't Factor;
2. The Strange Order, or, Everything-Is-Paradoxical Factor; and
3. The Weird Connections, or, Everything-Is-Interconnected-in-Strange-Ways Factor.

Taken together, they explain why reality is so generally bewildering. They reveal that we are no longer, as we once were, in control of our destiny. In a nutshell, we are now the prisoner of, or at the very least subjected to, powerful and distant forces beyond our complete control. The reader should be cautioned that there is no clear-cut dividing line between these factors. All shade into one another.

Factor One: The Failure of Success

To understand the complexity that constitutes the new reality, the proper starting point is the condition in which the U.S. found itself immediately after World War II.[1] Then the U.S. was the richest, strongest, biggest, and most productive economy in the world, its factories the most modern with the latest manufacturing technologies. Its workforce was the best educated and most productive. Its industry produced the most advanced and highest quality goods. As a result, U.S. goods were in high demand. In return for their high productivity and the high demand for goods, U.S. workers enjoyed the highest salary benefits and standard of living anywhere on the planet.

All of this was made possible by a number of distinct advantages the U.S. enjoyed over almost all other economies and nations of the world.

One, our resource base was incredible, the U.S. being blessed unlike no other nation in the abundance and extent of its raw materials. With very few exceptions, the U.S. was nearly self-sufficient. It was independent, as few nations were, of having to call upon the raw materials of others.

Two, its internal domestic markets were so huge, and relatively speaking, so unsaturated of goods and services of all kinds, especially after the deprivation years of the war, that for all practical purposes U.S. manufacturers and businesses could ignore without harm all other foreign markets and concentrate almost exclusively on markets they not only knew more intimately but could control more fully and directly.

Three, our general technology base was the latest and

most advanced, thus making our entire society the most modern for the times.

Four, the U.S. had in effect an almost monopolistic lock on the importation of whatever raw materials it lacked and at a cost considerably below prevailing world prices. Because the rest of the world lacked the productive and manufacturing facilities, they had few choices but to ship their raw materials to the U.S. below prevailing world market prices in return for final, finished products that were sold back to them.

Five, the U.S. had one of the finest infrastructures mankind had ever seen. Its road, highway, communication, and educational systems were the best for the times.

Six, consumers not only were starved for goods after the war, but found their tastes relatively standardized and homogeneous. This meant that manufacturers could produce a limited number of distinct types and styles of goods, knowing that what they produced would be gobbled up instantly, no questions asked.

Seven, consumer tastes were also rather predictable and stable, i.e., long lasting. For example, some 40 years ago, the life cycle of a typical consumer product like, say, a refrigerator was normally 30 years. A new product first would be bought by the early adopters, i.e., the avant-garde, the opinion leaders, the wealthy, the experimental, etc. Then, as costs came down, it would slowly diffuse its way through the rest of the population until its adoption was nearly complete, except for induced demand through yearly model changes. All this meant that it was relatively easy to justify the costs involved in building big plants and equipment that were necessary to produce the goods in large quantities to service mass markets. One could be relatively certain that the demand for goods would still be there by the time they rolled off the assembly lines into American stores.

Eight, the costs of transporting raw materials, finished goods, services, information, and even knowledge itself between countries were relatively high. Thus, the two oceans acted as natural and, even more important, as one-way buffers. Since we were stronger and, so we perceived, smarter than the rest of the world, we could penetrate markets anywhere if we desired. (For the most part we were content not to.) But the huge costs involved prevented foreign manufacturers from setting up factories, distribution and dealer networks on our home shore. The grand result was that in effect we could ignore the rest of the world, but they could not ignore us. We *were* the world. We not only wrote its songs, but literally called the tune and choreographed the dance steps.

Nine, bigness was pursued almost indefinitely, i.e., without limit, and solely for its own sake. Indeed, bigness followed almost axiomatically from the other conditions or advantages we possessed. If the U.S. had a decisive advantage in brains, talent, Yankee ingenuity, a well educated and large labor force, a rich abundance of relatively cheap raw materials, and further consumer tastes that were quite predictable, enduring and stable, then manufacturing organizations—and even government agencies—could grow, so it would seem, almost without limit and lose no efficiency in the process. The plain fact was that for the times organizations could by growing bigger achieve greater efficiencies and economies of scale, and they did precisely this for several decades. Who after all could argue against big government and big business when in close partnership they had just successfully fought the largest war in history? Thus, like the land itself that was so big that it seemingly could never fully be conquered, organizations pursued growth like a demon. They aimed to be as expansive as the land they strove to emulate and finally to conquer. In a word, the U.S. became the biggest, most successful economic engine—machine—the world had ever seen. And the term "machine," metaphor that it is, was the perfect description for the country.

From its very beginnings, America had always had a deep and lasting love affair with technology. The country's true religion was always the belief in progress, especially progress aided by technology. If progress was the ultimate shining light of American society, then technology was its guiding hand-servant. And what better conception of a stable, smoothly running world, all of whose inputs were under control (raw materials, labor, infrastructure, consumer tastes and demand), than a "machine"?

Given the overwhelming success and advantages the U.S. enjoyed, what possibly could ever happen to derail the American dream machine? Or had there always been a monster, a nightmare, lurking somewhere within it? The answer is not only "yes," but it can be given a definite name: *The Failure of Success.*

Ironically, it was not the initial failure of the American experiment itself that led to the difficulties that the U.S. is currently experiencing. Rather, it was America's huge, unparalleled successes. Or more precisely, it was the country's enormous failure as a culture to understand that it was only a very special, limited set of conditions that made for America's temporary success no matter how long they seemed to last. In a word, we confused and took for granted short time, temporary, *conditions* as permanent, God-granted *advantages* that existed for all time. We failed to understand and to take the necessary corrective actions to prevent nearly every single one of our crushing advantages from turning into crushing disadvantages.

While we rested on our laurels after World War II, the other nations of the world, their economic and infrastructures either destroyed or undeveloped, had nowhere to go but up. Indeed, the U.S. itself even became one of the biggest contributing factors to the rebuilding of the other economies through the Marshall Plan and like aid programs.

To understand The Failure of Success, let's review how nearly every one of what were once decisive advantages for the U.S. turned into disadvantages. Japan, for one, had no choice but to rebuild its almost totally destroyed manufacturing base after World War II. Further, unlike the U.S. which had always been blessed with an overabundance of cheap raw materials, Japan had always been faced with a general impoverishment of raw materials. Thus, when Japan rebuilt its manufacturing base, it did so not only with the next generation of even more modern and more efficient plants and facilities, but along the lines that would squeeze the most advantages out of a limited raw material base. Even more astounding, Japan learned how to turn its meager raw material base, i.e., its disadvantages, into crushing advantages.

Unlike the U.S. which possessed such a wealth of raw materials it could literally afford to squander them in industrial processes that in a relatively few years after the war were becoming increasingly more inefficient because of their bigness and advancing age, Japan had no choice but to opt for processes that conserved energy and materials in the most efficient manner possible. Such processes usually meant the construction of a larger number of smaller factories; Japan's mini steel mills are just the latest developments in this long line of thinking and experimentation. But smallness, it turned out, also possessed other decisive advantages as well. By building smaller, more efficient plants, the Japanese, as well as the Koreans, and later the Taiwanese, were learning other invaluable lessons about flexibility and interdependence that would serve them extremely well some 25 years later. They were learning that on every dimension and every level of society, "less can be more."

Since smaller plants were easier to design, maintain, and manage than big ones, they permitted much more flexible manufacturing processes that were capable of shifting quickly from one production mode to another. Thus, in the '70s and '80s when consumer tastes not only became more differentiated and segmented but changed literally overnight in response to the latest fashions and fads, the Japanese learned how to shift production runs to accommodate those tastes more quickly than did the Americans. (Other nations quickly learned how to follow suit. The success of the Benetton stores is only one of many dramatic examples, with their sales outlets linked all over the world via computers. This means it has become literally possible to orchestrate overnight style and color changes that would have boggled the mind a decade ago. To do this means of course that Benetton's management has had to forge extremely close ties with the clothing mills in order to produce at a favorable cost savings the latest fashions that are at the leading edge of what consumers want—or can be made to want.)

The ability to quickly shift production runs proved to be an extremely important asset as the cost of transporting huge volumes of raw materials, information, and knowledge long distances decreased enormously. This meant that the great distances and geographical barriers between nations were no longer the natural buffers they had been for so long. This in turn allowed foreign manufacturers to invade more quickly and effectively the home turf of their domestic competition. With quicker and cheaper means of transporting huge quantities of information via computer, foreign companies could more easily communicate with their offshore plants and facilities. It was easier than ever to establish nationwide transportation and dealer networks overseas. The U.S., having always relied on its huge internal domestic markets as being inpenetrable, was now at a considerable disadvantage. It knew only how to sell efficiently to one market. Its manufacturing and plant facilities were not only rapidly becoming out of date, and hence inefficient, but increasingly inflexible as well. The result was that U.S. manufacturers could not even keep up with the constantly shifting tastes of their own consumers, losing market share in world markets in which they once had enjoyed commanding leads (for example, in the '50s the U.S. had nearly 50 percent of world steel markets whereas its share is now 30 percent and heading lower;[2] for another, the Japanese now produce a larger total volume of cars than we do, a situation that would have been unimaginable just two short decades ago). They were also in danger of losing significant shares of their own internal markets. By not learning how to market and to compete globally as the Japanese, by necessity, had to learn the U.S. lost ground in its domestic as well as international markets.

No one would wish on any country a devastating war. But if there was anything good that came out of World War II from the Japanese standpoint, it was that they had no place to go but up and that meant a total overhaul of their entire manufacturing apparatus. The point is that when one's total infrastructure is destroyed, the ground for accomplishing significant change is made infinitely easier. Crisis, as we have had to learn again and again, may be the best, if not the only, teacher on how to overhaul an economy so that it is better matched to the needs of today's world.

All of which leads inevitably to interdependency. If Japanese firms were to reap the advantages of smallness (e.g., the ability to shift and to adapt quickly to changing consumer tastes), then they had to coordinate the efforts of innumerable groups both inside and outside the boundaries of their organizations. For example, if the Japanese were to cut the tremendous costs of holding huge amounts of raw materials and finished products in inventory, then they had to reduce the size of their factories. But this meant that they had to forge close ties with their external suppliers whom they could trust to deliver the right materials at the right time and in the right spots daily and in many cases hourly. American factories have always been big stockpilers of parts and finished products, since the cost of buying and maintaining land had never been as expensive as it was in Japan. For another, American manufacturers could never fully trust their suppliers and dealers as well as the Japanese could. Indeed, the relationships between suppliers and manufacturers was often as adversarial as it was between management and labor. The story is often told that in the '30s and '40s one could walk through the plants of the big three auto companies in Detroit and literally smell food emanating from the washrooms. Apparently relations between labor and management had deteriorated so seriously that the latter promulgated one emasculating rule after another, and in turn workers flaunted their contempt by running on company time small restaurants and barbershops on plant facilities.

The divisiveness between labor and management was another problem that Japan had learned to avoid by forging more benign, less acrimonious relations among all the segments of their society. America had always been the quintessential land of *in*dependence, Japan of *inter*dependence. Because American factories could not count on the right parts (let alone quality ones) being delivered to the right place at the right time, they became huge holding pens of raw materials and finished products so that they could ride out whatever ups and downs appeared in both the input and output sides of the manufacturing process.

As incredible as it seemed at the time, this country's domestic markets did finally become saturated for traditional goods. True, there is always a continuing market for refrigerators, cars, TV sets, VCRs and the like. But the point is that such markets are mostly mature by now; they're not the same as they were in the beginning of the introduction of a new device. But more importantly still, consumer tastes have become so finely tuned and differentiated that it's becoming all but impossible to sell one kind of anything to everybody. The explosion in styles and varieties of running shoes is just one example. Who could have ever foreseen that the basic black and white gym model would have ever subdivided into so many different types?

As if the proliferation of different varieties of products were not enough, the life cycles of all products began to shrink to virtually zero. With the increased sophistication of mass marketing techniques, products diffuse faster and faster through the entire population. But this raises an incredible dilemma for all businesses. How does one plan for products whose life cycles may be considerably shorter than the planning or production times involved in making them and getting them to the marketplace? How does one insure that there will still be a demand for one's products by the time they have been delivered to the marketplace? What in short does one do when consumer tastes can shift faster than the times involved in planning, producing, and distributing products?

With the spread of the modern computer, not only information traveled freely, but knowledge as well. The undeveloped economies of the Third World as well as the smaller economies of our allies learned some critical if not invaluable lessons. They found that instead of exporting their raw materials to us and importing back finished products, they could buy instead the necessary technology to convert their raw materials into finished products on their own shores which they could then sell cheaper than us to the rest of the world, as well as to themselves. Part of the reason is that their much cheaper labor costs are more than enough to offset the cost of transporting goods long distances, a cost which had been steadily decreasing anyway. Another factor was that societies other than our own learned from our experience and the learning increased exponentially. We were no longer on the leading edge of technology and of management expertise. The Japanese, Koreans, Taiwanese, and Brazilians, among many, were learning how to design and to manage entirely new kinds of industrial enterprises for which we were no longer the models. We forgot one of the critical lessons from which we started on the path of our industrial prowess. In the beginning, we copied the British much like the Japanese have aped us. We then used our Yankee ingenuity to tinker, to improve on, the inventions of others much as others were now improving on ours. We were struggling to learn a painful lesson; we were no longer the center of the universe. It's a lesson that no former empire ever finds easy to learn.

Of all the advantages we enjoyed just immediately following World War II, perhaps nothing was as critical to the disadvantages we now confront as one factor in particular: bigness. Whereas once bigness in itself connoted and led to further strength and advantage, increasingly on every front of our existence, bigness led to inefficiency, ineffectiveness, and even weakness. What happened was that the underlying infrastructure of the world has evolved so radically that in effect the basic rules of the game changed altogether.

Consider the matter this way. If the world were indeed a machine, and a simple one at that, then its understanding, design, and operation would be rather straightforward. For hadn't the Industrial Revolution taught us, if not convinced us, that everything in the world was like a machine including man himself, and hence explainable in machine-like terms? Since one of the prime properties of machines is that they can be broken apart, reduced to, and hence ultimately built from decomposable parts, wasn't the same therefore true of man and of all his institutions? Wasn't the human body decomposable as well into separate component parts or centers which had nearly autonomous existences of their own? Indeed, wasn't knowledge itself subdividable like the different parts of a machine so that it could be neatly codified into separate autonomous disciplines? And finally, didn't we learn from the great German sociologist Max Weber that organizations themselves were machines so that if one part failed to work well, the defective part merely had to be pulled out and replaced with a new one?

One of the most appealing properties of the world if it were a machine is that the greater the inputs into it, the greater the resulting outputs. And generally speaking this is true *if* the machine is able to maintain the same level of output efficiency no matter what the size of the material that is input into it.

Unfortunately, human institutions do not fit this general pattern. (Neither do physical machines in general, but that's another matter.) What we find increasingly on every front of human existence is that greater inputs into human organizations do not result in greater outputs or benefits. First of all, in order to handle greater inputs, human organizations generally have to become bigger, and bigger organizations are generally more inefficient than smaller ones. (This is not always necessarily the case, nor does it have to be, but only if we are willing to expend greater energy in getting the organization's members to work together better, the larger the organization becomes. Without greater cohesiveness and understanding between the members of an organization, the larger it gets generally the more inefficient it becomes.) Thus, the mergers of more and more organizations into fewer bigger ones that in turn begot even larger organizations, private as well as public, right after World War II led to their generally increased inefficiency.[3]

When it became coupled with the increased world interdependency in turn aided by the modern computer revolution, bigness led to a final result which broke once and for all the lock that the simple conception of the world as a machine had on society's mind. It is well known that all processes have an upper limit to their efficiency. At some point bigness boomerangs and turns back on itself. Instead of leading to greater end benefits, it produces negative end effects and possibly unforeseeable negative benefits that go completely counter to the hypothesized benefits of bigness. Thus, instead of "bigger being better" or "more inputs into the machine leading to bigger desired outputs," more or bigger inputs into an inefficient machine generally leads to less.

Factor Two: Paradox, Why Increasingly "More Leads to Less" on Every Front of Our Existence[4]

This point is so important that we need to explore it further, through looking at the complexities that are involved in the writing of the huge computer program that is needed to run Ronald Reagan's Star Wars Initiative (SDI). What emerges from this examination is the following. Once one reaches the ability to affect the whole globe, weird things begin to happen. *Actions that in the small or in isolation are good can have reverse, completely counterintuitive effects when they are magnified up to the level of affecting the whole globe.*

It is estimated that SDI will require a computer program roughly up to 100 times bigger than anything that has been written thus far, or approximately *ten to 100 million lines of computer instructions.* The program needed is so big because it must perform the innumerable calculations necessary to make the decision as to which enemy missiles to shoot down during which point in their flight paths, and thereby presumably make us more secure through a greater *defensive* capability rather than *offensive* capability.

Anyone who has ever created a computer program knows it is virtually impossible to write one, no matter how short it is, that will work perfectly the first time. Imagine then the "bugs" or imperfections in a program as huge as ten to 100 million lines! Here's precisely where counterintuitive effects begin to enter in, so strongly, in fact, that they illustrate a fundamental paradox characteristic of the complexity that constitutes our current environment. It is precisely the emergence of this paradox in every field of human endeavor that constitutes the complexity of the new reality.

One way to test the effectiveness of the computer program that is needed to run a Star Wars is to send up a wave of our own missiles whose trajectories we know precisely. (At some point, we have to test the program against actual missiles. If not we'd be dependent on another computer program to test the first one, and then we'd have to have supreme confidence in the second one to validate the first, etc., etc., etc.) Hence, we can then test the effectiveness of the program in shooting down missiles whose paths we presumably know since they are intentionally sent up. However, to really test the program to its limits we'd have to send up a *sizable swarm* of missiles because that's presumably what the U.S.S.R. would do during a real strike.

Query: How do we assure the Russians that the test swarm is only a *simulation* and not a first strike directed towards them? In order for *them* (the U.S.S.R.) to go along with *us* (the U.S.), they would have to trust us, the very quality that initially has been missing or we would not have been able to get SDI through our political system. Hence, the paradox is: The *less trust* there is between us and our adversaries, the *more* we build weapons of *bigger* scope (whether they are defensive or offensive); as a consequence, however, such weapons are *more complex* and therefore require *more extensive test* procedures; but such procedures necessitate greater (i.e., *more*) end trust and cooperation between us and our adversaries in order to carry out the test. But then why should they cooperate with us to further a weapon that is to their disadvantage? Notice that this discussion also makes clear why on the scale of global issues the whole distinction between "defensive" and "offensive" weapons collapses because of our need to send up a large swarm of our offensive missiles to test a supposedly purely defensive system; simpleminded distinctions are no longer viable at this level.

(The situation is even worse than this. For this country to really test the system, the Soviets would have to cooperate with us even further. They'd have to agree to send up an unarmed swarm of *their* missiles. If not, then we'd have to make the critical assumption that a swarm of our missiles would behave the same as a swarm of theirs. The two swarms may indeed be the same but with so much riding on this assumption, one should at least be aware that one is literally staking one's fate on it.)

The attempt to secure a decisive advantage or security through technology alone is self-defeating because the testing of the resultant technology depends upon political trust and cooperation from the adversary, the very thing that was missing in the first place and hence prompted the creating of the technology! But if such trust and cooperation are missing initially, where and how do they magically appear subsequently, especially, God forbid, in the heat of war, an extreme state that does not exactly contribute to the building of additional trust. *No one* has been able to answer this key question.

The point is that managing complexity calls for unconventional, new thinking of the highest order. It requires the ability to appreciate paradox and the fact that complex systems have multiple, diverse aspects so that they do not always follow traditional patterns such as "bigger is better." Those who see only one dimension of complex problems are now so out of touch with reality that they are truly dangerous. The failure to appreciate wider perspectives literally threatens our existence.

Because these points are admittedly difficult and yet vital to appreciate if we are to understand what's so changed about the nature of today's environment, we want to give another example, especially one that applies to the world of business. It reveals that few actions can be undertaken anymore without thinking through as clearly as possible their end effects. Further, since it's obviously impossible to anticipate everything, the best that can be done is to design policies and systems with as much flexibility built into them as possible so that as effects begin to emerge that are counter to those that were intended, the policies can be changed.

Recently an article appeared in *Business Week* entitled "Is Deregulation Working?," the whole point of which was that deregulation which was supposed to lead to greater productivity and competition through the removal of government regulations has actually produced the reverse effect. The entire example illustrates how instead of "more leading to more," i.e., more *de*regulation, supposedly a good thing, leading to an even *better* operation of the free market, just the reverse effect has resulted; of how more can lead to less *if* one doesn't have an understanding of the whole system in which everything now functions. *Unless the complexities of the whole system are taken into account, something which in isolation appears good can have the complete reverse, opposite, of the intended effects.*

The reason why more or greater deregulation didn't work the intended way is as follows. A chief goal of deregulation was to break up the cozy cartels that supposedly flourished under regulation. By breaking these cartels down, there supposedly would be an introduction of new competitors into markets. And in the beginning, there's no question that there was. In the end, however, the power that the big established players had, derived largely from their *extensive networks* (i.e., systems) of transportation and telecommunications facilities. If anything, these networks have expanded even more under deregulation by their acquisition of and linking up with smaller players. What happened is that those who fashioned the whole deregulation move vastly underestimated how much these huge networks served as barriers preventing others from getting into the game. As *Business Week* said, "Network owners enjoyed economies of flow or density, which are similar to the more familiar economies of scale in that average costs decline as network traffic increases. This gives the owner of a large network a clear cost advantage over a small network owner—and enormous market clout."

To quote *Business Week* again, "The networks themselves...have become competitive barriers almost as formidable as those erected by the regulators. Airline hub-in-spoke systems are obvious examples. An airline will use connecting flights to and from smaller spoke cities to generate traffic for flights from hubs in larger cities. Many small players find that the best way to survive is to collaborate with the big guys. Large airlines are buying and forming alliances with regional carriers and commuter airlines flying spoke routes into their hubs."[5]

To appreciate all of this requires precisely what has been called for from more than one presidential candidate. Namely, *new thinking. The ability to understand and to appreciate complexity and paradox is the quintessential essence of the new thinking we have been discussing. It calls for the ability to see broad patterns that influence our world and to avoid getting caught up in irrelevant details.*

The tragedy is that just when such broad understanding is of vital importance, particularly to understand why the old patterns that have governed the world for so long (i.e., bigger is better) no longer work, instead what we have gotten is more, narrow-trained, incapacity. Just when we need leadership even more on every front, we have gotten managership. As we have needed people who can dream big dreams and set even bigger goals for us, what we have gotten instead are bureaucrats who lack the basic ability to dream any dreams whatsoever and to see any broad patterns whatsoever.

It is almost as if when we needed a different kind of understanding to cope with complexity, even if it could no longer be fully tamed because such taming like understanding was completely impossible for any one single person, we have produced bureaucrats, the end results of a system that was designed to flee from reality. Hence, the circle became complete. *The characteristic features of the new reality are in near complete opposition to the characteristic features of the new unreality.* (In the next chapter, we contrast the features of reality and unreality more fully.)

Is it too much to really posit then that as reality became more complex, so complex that no one single individual could understand all the forces and patterns unleashed, we retreated more and more into the invention and proliferation of self-contained worlds of unreality over which we could maintain the illusion of control?

Factor Three: Weird Connections

What we have been driving at can be summarized in a single proposition: We've lost, perhaps once and for all, whatever slack and buffering we had built into our system. When we had huge, unsaturated domestic markets that were hungry for anything we could throw at them and hence didn't give much of a damn for goods and products that were different from what the Joneses next door wanted, we could get away with equally huge, bureaucratic organizations and production lines that were sloppy or inefficient. We could tolerate friction and hostility between labor, management, government, and stockholders. The problem today is that we can't get by any longer with this kind of behavior. We're competing with countries that make quality goods because they have forged close *alliances* among their employees, managers, governments, share-holders. They may not be perfect alliances but they stand in sharp contrast to our adversarial relationships. We were shielded from the rest of the world by temporary advantages which have now passed on to others.

An example is helpful. An article on the front page of the business section of the *Washington Post* brought forcefully home just how much our world has changed. It had to do with the fact that the U.S. and the worldwide travel industry really took it "in the shorts" the last couple of years. The obvious reasons have to do with the threat of terrorism and the fear that this has raised in travelers so that they were not as desirous of visiting abroad. That part of the reason for the trouble of the travel industry one can readily understand. It was the next part, having to do with the fact that travelers also stayed away from Europe because of Chernobyl, i.e., the fear of nuclear radiation, that really drove home once again how and why our world has changed so dramatically.

Imagine if you will this scenario. Suppose that, say three years ago, we had assembled a small conference of 50 people in one room, 25 from the travel industry and 25 from the nuclear industry. We said to them in effect that a significant event will happen in the nuclear industry that will greatly affect the travel. You know what would have happened? Both groups would have looked not only at one another in complete surprise, but at us as though we were crazy and had just descended from Mars with a banana in our ears.

The point is that the world is now governed by a condition of WEIRD CONNECTIONS! *Any two of the most improbable events that anyone can think of can now criss cross and connect up in weird and unpredictable ways that almost defy any person's imagination.* There is no separation anymore between any parts of the globe. Everything everywhere is now in effect local news.

The Chernobyl disaster shows how totally interconnected we've become. For instance, it took about two weeks for the *physical* cloud of radiation from Chernobyl to encircle the earth to contaminate fish on opposite sides of the globe. But it took only half a day for the world's *financial* markets to react to Chernobyl. The reason is that if the "bread basket" of the Soviet Union were knocked out of commission for God knows how long, what would that do to the futures for grain markets in the U.S. and Europe? The point is that our financial markets reacted almost instantaneously to Chernobyl because we're literally now wired electronically to every part and every event in the whole planet. Events like Chernobyl are capable of not only *physically* affecting the whole planet, but also *electronically* and *financially* as well. This is a whole new level of affecting human events that we've never experienced before. We are now more coupled to distant forces beyond our complete control than we have ever been.

Since 1900, there have been 28 major industrial accidents in the world of the kind now indicated by Bhopal.[6] With Chernobyl the number has now grown. By "major" is meant the deaths of 50 people or more (not counting airplane crashes or natural disasters). The estimates are that Chernobyl will exceed this number by hundreds if not thousands of deaths over the coming years. The clinker in the preceding statistic is that since 1900 not only have there been 29 major industrial accidents, but *half* of these have occurred after 1980! The point is the ante not only keeps going up, i.e., the disasters we are witnessing are not only bigger in scope, but the time between them is shrinking precipitously. Worse yet, each type of disaster keeps breaking the records for its class. Thus Tylenol is the biggest product tampering incident of its kind to date; Bhopal,

Chernobyl, the Space Shuttle, the crash of the stock market, and the latest, the spilling of oil in Alaska, are the biggest of their kind.

The whole structure of our world has changed fundamentally. We doubt seriously that a poisoning incident of the type represented by Tylenol would have happened some 60 years ago. The kind of accidents we had then were no less devastating to a particular community but the point is that they were mainly *confined to* a particular community. A disaster like a mine explosion for instance could wipe out and be catastrophic to a particular community, but it wouldn't have affected a *whole nation* or a whole region. The reason why a product tampering, for instance, can happen today is that we have the mixed blessings of modern communications and travel technology. With mass communication and mass transportation, a single psychopath can get on a plane and, unfortunately, visit five cities in a day. Hence, when somebody calls in to a company with a product tampering threat, we really have no choice but to take the idea of a nationwide product recall very seriously unless we can determine that the so-called tampering threat, if indeed it is real to begin with, was confined to a particular locale or a particular batch of products, a task that is increasingly difficult, in a complex system. How does one locate the particular bottle of poisoned products out of hundreds of thousands of containers (or grapes) scattered across a continent?

No wonder paradox operates in today's world. No one can foresee all the complex interconnectedness of everything, that everything is both weakly and strongly interconnected at the same time. The weakness is that there are so many potential connections between things that few are permanently or directly connected all the time. At the same time, the strength is that if any two things do connect up, then the effect is often instantaneous and dramatic. Thus, even though one starts out assuming that what one is doing is good, it can have adverse effects. Things are now so complex that actions that seem good can lead to the complete opposite of what one had intended.

An example of the phenomenon we have been discussing is what happened to the stock market on October 19th, 1987. Experts believe that one of the biggest factors responsible for the crash of the market that Monday was the behavior of the computerized trading programs. Very simply put, the computer programs are designed to make certain buy and sell decisions in order to protect individual investors when particular stock indices go below certain levels (sell) or go above others (buy). The paradox is that the programs which were initially designed to protect individual investors from the impact of sharp declines helped to cause those very declines by speeding up selling when markets declined sharply. That is, the programs helped not only to create the phenomenon they were supposedly designed to protect against but to speed it up and exacerbate its effects as well. Once again, we witness the emergence of "more leads to less" and where it unfortunately affects every one of us, in our pocketbooks. Or to put the paradox in terms we have been discussing: The ability to make more and faster selling decisions which was supposedly to confer more or greater protection for individual investors actually led to less protection, i.e., their being less well off. The reason is that the programs failed to take adequately into account how the stock market *as a whole system* would function collectively if the investment decisions of sizable numbers of people were guided by the same programs in different investment firms; in effect, more led to less because of the failure once again to consider effects on the whole system. As Stewart Brand has put it:

> New technologies create new freedoms and new dependencies. The freedoms are more evident at first. The dependencies may never become evident, which makes them all the worse, because then it takes a crisis to discover them. Crises of large complex systems can be nasty, if the system hasn't had time to mature a lot of checks and balances.[7]

Concluding Remarks

Richard Schickel has observed wisely that an appreciation for complexity has always been regarded as a sign of
weakness by the masses who have no taste whatsoever for
it. Which is now to say that reality itself must be regarded
as the ultimate sign of weakness by the masses, for reality
has become virtually synonymous with complexity. Little
wonder then why as a result we should have become
preoccupied with a Flight From Reality through the creation of multiple forms of unreality. It is to a more detailed
look at the mechanisms that underlie the production and
creation of unreality to which we now turn.

3. Boundary Warping
Unreality's Primary Mechanism

SCENE I: A TV camera zooms in on a globe suspended in space. The U.S. hurtles into prominence. Images of a particular state, then a region, and finally a specific city come into focus. Suddenly, the scene shifts to an attractive couple seated behind an impressive looking desk. Behind them is an even larger, spectacular set. Both the man and the woman are well dressed. They seem to be smiling all the time. Not only are they well groomed but they reflect the confidence of polished performers who are at ease in front of the camera. They patter back and forth. While the dialogue is not quite at the level of Bruce Willis and Cybill Shepherd, that's obviously the model they are striving for.

SCENE II: We see mothers and young kids waiting in a pediatrician's office. In the background is a giant video screen that literally takes up most of the wall. On it can be found several high paced, action commercials for the latest creations from the toy manufacturers. The stuff is heavy paced and makes no bones about the fact that it was produced to do one thing and one thing only: sell toys. The

toys pictured are the latest hi-tech, prosthetically enhanced, superheroes that are capable of transforming
instantly into other objects and other creatures. Some of
the videos actually allow the kids to interact directly with
them by shooting guns or pointing laser beams. The
message underlying all of the presentations is clear: on
every conceivable scale, humans are weaker, less intelligent,
and less skilled than their technological counterparts. Also,
buy our products and maybe you'll become a super hero
too!

SCENE III: A television special appears on Monday, October
12, 1987, during prime time on ABC. It's a star-studded
celebration of the 200th anniversary of the United States
Constitution. The program is co-produced by Richard
Dreyfuss who also hosts the extravaganza. A cavalcade of
stars from Lily Tomlin, Whoopi Goldberg and Randy
Newman to Henry Winkler and Sir John Gielgud appears.
Jiminy Cricket, Donald Duck and Mickey Mouse make
cameo appearances. The program is a slick fast-paced
entertaining melange of special effects, electronic graphics,
cartoon images, and "real people." The program succeeds
in reducing the story and the meaning of the Constitution
to a Saturday morning kids' cartoon. Given the format of
the program, with Dreyfuss functioning as intelligently as
one could as master of ceremonies, it nonetheless displays
one of TV's central discoveries/inventions: all images are
created equal. Thus, the ruminations of a Mickey Mouse on
the U.S. Constitution are as profound, as important, and as
convincing as those of a Lily Tomlin, which makes sense of
course if one accepts the proposition that in TV-land there
are no essential differences between a Mickey and a Lily.

Fantasy? Not quite! Scene I is the background to the
morning and evening news programs which pervade
America. Scene II is not quite yet reality in all its aspects,
but it's close enough to be frightening. When all boundaries are erased and up for sale, what is there to prevent
the selling of products anywhere and everywhere in contemporary America? Scene III is a synopsis of a program
that has actually appeared. It demonstrates another of
TV's prime discoveries/inventions: everything that appears

in the medium is a subdivision of the realm of entertainment.

Welcome to Boundary Warping, one of unreality's primary mechanisms.

In the early days of radio, advertisers discovered an important device—a trick if you will—for getting audiences to listen to commercials. Advertisers discovered that audiences would not only listen to commercials but, more important, not complain about their disrupting effects if they were cleverly woven into the normal dialogue of the program. Thus, on many of the popular shows of the day, for example, Jack Benny, Fibber McGee and Molly, Burns and Allen, etc., the characters would more or less subtly, and sometimes overtly, begin to tout some advertiser's product as part of the show's normal routine, act, story line, etc. Most often, the transitions between the programs and the commercials themselves were so subtle that the audience would not be aware, or be able to tell, briefly that what they were listening to was a commercial as distinct from the normal program. The audience would get carried along by the believability of the plot characters, especially their likeability, which of course was exactly what the advertisers intended. Few, if any, howls of protest or outrage accompanied this development. For the most part, it was greeted by no reaction at all. After all, what real harm was done? Didn't the sponsors after all pay for the program? Weren't the stars in their employ? Couldn't the products be advertised in a manner the sponsors saw fit as long as listeners weren't offended?

The J. Walter Thompson Agency, a deft experimenter in the techniques of interweaving, discovered a technique in 1929 for involving listeners and for creating a kind of "plot," even in a musical variety show. The show was set in a club. During a simulated intermission the host, crooner Rudy Vallee, sauntered among the tables introducing his guest to fans until they happened to overhear a conversation at one table. Vallee said, "Let's listen," to his friend (and to the radio audience). A change in tone quality signaled a change in microphone; then the radio listener found himself joining Vallee in eavesdropping on a young couple who were marveling at the man's great success in business since he had been taking Fleischmann's Yeast. Advertisers had already recognized the power of the "overheard conversation" to induce reader involvement...Here was a demonstration that radio was a more natural medium than print for luring the consumer into a conspiracy to eavesdrop. The listener became the host's unwitting accomplice in a trick that suddenly shifted the scene from entertainment to a commercial vignette. Having assented to the initial titillation of eavesdropping, the consumer could not even plead entrapment.[1]

Important events and/or trends often have such seemingly innocuous starts. Who could have foreseen that such inauspicious beginnings would lead to something more serious? Or that over a long period of time the gradual, deepening intrusion or crossover of commercials into program content would desensitize us to the occurrence of the phenomenon itself and contribute to our inability to see its true seriousness? Who after all could have foreseen that the eventual crossover of commercials would become so serious that parents would at last complain that the Saturday morning kids' shows were in effect half-hour long commercials devoid of almost any wholesome content whatsoever and produced solely for the purpose of getting kids to buy expensive toys? Further still, who could have foreseen that these earlier crossover attempts were in effect primitive, mostly subconscious, social experiments that would lead eventually to the crossover between much more serious lines such as news as entertainment as we discussed briefly in Chapter One? No, all this would have perhaps been beyond the ability of even the most astute social observer to have detected at the time.

This short example reveals that unreality has a long and complex history, that the phenomenon does not spring forth full blown. Like most important social phenomena, it begins in innocent appearing ways. If this were a more complete treatment of the subject, we would recount this long history in detail. We would show that one person's reality is another's unreality, that the reality of one age is the unreality of another:

> Now that radio had descended to the popular level, the comic-strip technique provided an effective means for creating advertising "tie-ins" among the media. Several advertisers translated the radio-program characters into the protagonist of their comic-strip copy in magazines and newspapers and on product packages. In this way, readers of their print advertising could be converted into part of the audience for the radio shows and vice versa. The "voice personality" of many radio characters was now linked to an engaging cartoon caricature. If advertising had "gone entertainment" as some critcis of the trends in radio and comic sections lamented, then entertainment figures, from comic-strip heroes to radio crooners and comedians, had reciprocated the gesture: they now animated products by infusing them with their own personalities.
>
> The new media of the 1920s and early 1930s taught a harsh lesson to advertising leaders who prided themselves on their rationality and seriousness of purpose. Nothing in the logic of modernization had suggested that big business should engage in "show business." But the popularity of the new medium demonstrated again and again...that the public preferred "the frivolous against the serious, 'escape' as against reality...the diverting as against the significant." Just as the newspaper reader chose the tabloid picture over the serious story and the comic page over the foreign news, and just as the radio audience tuned its style to tasteless comedy rather than classical music, so the consumer would not accept serious advice about products *in any medium* without a dream world of frivolity and fantasy to go with it. People seemed to want escapist fantasy, a feeling of personal identification with fictitious characters and celebrities, even more than they wanted products. Such a rationality was unfortunate, perhaps, and advertising agents liked to think that they did not share it. But it was an irrationality they could not afford to ignore.[2]

A complete treatment of the history of unreality, however, is not our goal. Our primary purpose instead is to reveal as fully as we can the differences between the reality and unreality of our times. Even more, our goal is to reveal the underlying mechanisms operating today to produce unreality. Our hope is that if we have a better understanding of how unreality is produced, then we may have a better chance of assessing both its influence and the possibility of its containment, if not reversal.

The short introductory example of the intrusion of radio commercials into program content is just one of the many mechanisms we are able to identify that are responsible for the production of unreality. Table 1 gives a full listing of what at this time we are able to identify as the primary mechanisms, plus a brief explanation of what they are and how they operate. Table 2, on the other hand, gives a brief explanation of the characteristic differences between reality and unreality. While there are sharp differences between the two, the latter table shows nonetheless that there are strong points of overlap between reality and unreality. This strong overlap does not mean that distinction between reality and unreality is useless or meaningless, but rather, like all important social phenomena, it is complex. Indeed, this is the basis for the claim that we made in Chapter One that at times the line between reality and unreality is vanishingly thin at best.

TABLE 1

The Mechanisms for Unreality Production

(1) *Boundary Warping*, i.e., the deliberate distortion and confusion between traditional realms of reality, for example, between entertainment and news; the general rule is that everything that appears on TV, and increasingly in every segment of our society, is a branch of entertainment;

(2) *Image Engineering*, i.e., any image that human beings are capable of imagining can now be constructed electronically and is capable of interacting with any other image; the general rules are: (a) all images are equal, and (b) the more bizarre the image, "the more equal," the "better" the image is; in Orwellian terms, some images are "more equal" than others;

(3) *Personality Fragmentation or Splitting of the Person*, ideas are not only split apart and rendered incoherent on TV and

increasingly on all forms of entertainment and communication in our society, but so are the various aspects of people; thus, isolated individual body parts (e.g., breasts, faces, noses, hair, and teeth, etc.) assume an identity of their own; further, individual aspects of the person's psyche (e.g., ego), specific emotions (e.g., greed, anger, love), or archetypal characters (e.g., the Warrior as in the movie *Conan the Barbarian*) are also isolated and treated out of any larger context that would relate to the whole person;

(4) *Person Engineering*, the general principle is that a specific person can be manufactured or made over to embody any set of personality characteristics determined by market research to be appealing to a significant segment of the population;

(5) *The Disconnectedness of Ideas*, on the surface at least, there is little, if any, connection between the ideas that float off TV or the other segments of our society; no connecting thread, overall context, or historical perspective is provided that would help the viewer, reader, audience, etc., make any sense of the larger pattern of ideas, images, etc., assuming that there was one, that would tie all of the images or ideas together into any coherent whole;

(6) *A Self-Sealing Universe*, the general principle is that TV and increasingly all the other forms of communication in our society, refer less and less to anything outside of their own artificially, self-constructed, self-contained world; the result is that virtually all of the forms of unreality have become almost totally capable of incorporating any criticism directed against them by including those very criticisms into their day to day operations; thus, TV shows and commercials of all kinds, for instance the popular Joe Isuzu ads, incorporate the very cynicism against the media into its operations;

(7) *Personality Reduction*, everything is personality on TV and in the general entertainment society of America; abstract ideas tend not to exist; they exist only if they can be represented in a concrete person; for example, Einstein is the personal embodiment of the intellectual, Joan Collins is the archetypal bitch, etc.;

(8) *Radical Simplification*, all forms of unreality have no room for abstract ideas; they have even less for complex ones; for instance, everything on TV and in popular books must be

simplified up to and beyond the point of trivialization; the result is TV and contemporary American culture not only constitute a vast wasteland on the landscape of history, but worse yet, they constitute one of the largest efforts in programmatic ignorance or unreality creation on the face of the planet;

(9) *Instant Means for Celebrityhood,* one of the most disturbing aspects of unreality is that the psychopath may understand better than those who supposedly have a grip on so-called "normal" reality the means for achieving instantaneous celebrityhood, i.e., the murder and assassination of someone else who is already a celebrity;

(10) *Reverse Causality,* TV has rendered traditional causality, i.e., the traditional sequence of events, irrelevent; TV sound plays a highly important role in this process; for this very reason, its role is often overlooked; TV sound summons the passive viewer/listener back to the set to watch a rewinding of an "important event"; e.g., first a touchdown (or an important political event, news story) is scored, then we watch in reverse sequence what "caused it," only the "cause" in this case now becomes the "effect";[3]

(11) *The Decentralized Industrial Stage of Unreality Production,* celebrities are the chief products of an entire industry and the industry has advanced to the next stage in its development; celebrities can now be literally manufactured from nearly any part of the country; it is no longer necessary to move to New York, L.A., or Nashville to name a few of the previously centralized locations from where celebrities could once only be produced;

(12) *Infrastructure Penetration and Contamination,* the manufacturing of unreality has reached such proportions that it has literally infiltrated itself into virtually every aspect of U.S. life; the phenomenon is thus so deeply and widely entrenched into the very lifeblood of U.S. society that its eradication is highly problematic at this point.

TABLE 2

SOME PRINCIPAL DIFFERENCES BETWEEN REALITY & UNREALITY

Characteristics	Reality	Unreality
1. Boundary Maintenance/Control	Breakdown/irrelevancy of traditional geopolitical, professional boundaries; inability to control/maintain traditional boundaries	Deliberate crossover/manipulation of traditional boundaries for profit and illusion of control
2. Public Awareness/Perceived Seriousness of Boundary Breakdown	Mixed: Indifference to Alarming	Low to little
3. Degree of Complexity	High	Low in Appearance
a. Number of Dimensions	Multiple	Reduction of all issues to a Single Overriding Dimension: Personality, Image, Celebrity
b. History Provided/Necessary for Understanding	Long, Complex	None, Little
c. Context Provided/Necessary for Understanding	High/Dependent	None, Little
d. Intellectual Demands Placed on the Average Citizen	Overwhelming	Oscillates Radically Between Overloading and Underwhelming
e. Connectedness Between Events, Places	Simultaneously Strong and Weak, Weird	Near Total Absence of Clear Connections, None Supplied
f. Background Knowledge/Prerequisites Needed to Make Sense of an Event	Severe/Taxing	None to Little
g. Degree/Clarity of Understanding Provided	Little: Paradoxical	Little: Trivial, Simplistic
h. Emotional State Induced	Invokes High Anxiety	Diverting, Amusing
i. Solubility of Problems	Unresolvable over Centuries	Disposed of in 30 Minutes or Less

Characteristics	Reality	Unreality
j. Pace/Flow of Events	Chaotic	Frenetic
4. Public Involvement/ Participation	Low	Low
a. Perceived control Over Events	Low	Mixed
5. Guarantors for Knowledge	Mixed: Political, Conflicting Experts, Scientific	Abundant Use of Fantasy, Deliberate Fabrication, Distortion of Facts

The radio example is illustrative of the first, and what we take to be the primary, mechanism for the production of unreality, Boundary Warping. Because of its importance, we devote this chapter primarily to its exploration by means of several examples. We examine some of the other mechanisms in more detail in later chapters, although the mechanisms themselves are so intertwined that in discussing one, we will inevitably be touching on the others. The reason for this goes back to Chapter Two.

The world is no longer a simple machine. Mechanisms and their effects no longer either exist or operate in isolation. Everything is part of a larger system. Everything is interconnected. The result is a much greater impact of any single mechanism than if it either existed or operated in isolation. If only one or two of the mechanisms in Table 1 existed, then they probably could be absorbed with little harm or notice by society. But when increasingly each reinforces the others, then the overall effect can be devastating.

Boundary Warping: Everything Is Now a Sub-branch of the Entertainment Division of the World

The lines between every conceivable field of human activity are becoming—or already have become—thinner and thinner and are rapidly approaching the vanishing point. Thus, for instance, the lines between politics, entertainment, religion, business, education, and the law—you

name it—have been all eroded to the point where it has
become less and less possible to say where any one field of
activity ends and another begins.

In itself, the blurring of boundaries is not necessarily
bad for the lines between all forms of human activity have
always been somewhat artificial and misleading at best and
outright false and dangerous at worst. Increasingly, there
are no clear lines between the professions. For example,
consider: (a) medicine and engineering which have now
joined together to form bio-engineering, and (b) medicine,
engineering, and ethics which have joined to form bio-
ethics. In both cases, the collapse between the boundaries
dividing these fields has occurred because new fields (bio-
engineering, bio-ethics) have had to be created in order to
handle the problems that arise on a nearly daily basis due
to our newfound abilities to prolong human life and to
create new life forms. Thus, the current blurring of
professional lines is in itself an important reflection of the
new *reality*, i.e., the increased complexity of the modern
world. The old distinctions and barriers between professions are no longer relevant to today's complex world. At
its best, Boundary Warping is an example of what has been
referred to positively by others as Boundary Elasticity.[4]
Under this concept, Boundary Elasticity is a positive way of
handling the complexity of the environment. The fact that
the news media allow events to literally explode off the
screen at viewers without prepackaging them into a single
coherent framework reflects the fact that democracy is
working. That the news media refuse to organize our
experience for us into a coherent framework is supposedly
a good thing. After all, the convenient organization of
experience into prearranged categories has always been a
prime characteristic of totalitarian regimes. Thus, the
refusal of the networks to organize our experience for us
not only gives them greater flexibility to cover events that
don't fit preassigned pigeonholes, but also supposedly
gives viewers greater flexibility to organize reality for
themselves even if such organization is disturbing and
provokes anxiety. Whether this is merely a convenient
rationalization or a positive virtue is of course a matter of

no small dispute. For instance, other societies, instead of providing no single framework or ideology for organizing experience, prefer to make TV time explicitly available for several different political parties to present or debate their interpretations of events.

What we find disturbing about Boundary Warping must refer therefore to something far more ominous, for what we humans call reality is always the product of somewhat arbitrary distinctions. In fact, a working definition of reality is that it *consists of all those sets of carefully negotiated and evolved distinctions between things that we find convenient for giving order to our world. Reality, in other words, marks off the boundaries between critical things, events, and processes.* For example, it's the dividing line between life and death, between living and nonliving things, between children and adults, between the fetus and the newborn, between the insane and the mentally competent, between the normal and the abnormal, between sanity and insanity, etc. In every case, strong elements of judgment and even some arbitrariness are present, for all distinctions are the products of human culture, and different cultures do not draw the same boundaries around things, especially those that are critical to everyday life.

What is it then that is so distinctive about Boundary Warping that it leads to unreality? Why do we call one form of blurring characteristic of the complexity that constitutes the new reality with which we are faced and another characteristic of unreality? Simply put, the difference refers to Pseudo Reality or what in Chapter One we called Unreality Two. *Unreality is the result of the massive infusion of entertainment into every realm of human affairs to the point that everything threatens to become nothing but a sub-branch of it.* Further, unreality occurs when everything not only becomes a sub-branch of entertainment but does so in such ways that we are not even aware that it has occurred. Thus, unreality is not only the subsumption of those fields of human activity that purport to deal with reality (i.e., complexity) under the rubric of entertainment but where the subsumption has been accomplished in such ways that the invasion of entertainment is denied, distorted, and generally kept invisible from the consuming public. In brief, *unreality results when complexity is denied and distorted by a society that is hooked on massive dosages of entertainment in order for it to function.*

We need to ground the discussion by means of a few examples beyond those that we presented in Chapter One. Three are especially pertinent: MTV, *The People's Court*, and the Saturday morning kids' shows.

Music Videos

In the realm of Boundary Warping, music videos are king.[5] The very essence of their structure is that of Boundary Warping.

The structure of music videos, MTV offering the prime example, is literally that of a dream.[6] Dreams generally have the following properties:

(1) There are no limits to the amounts of imagery contained within them; everything within a dream is symbolic and stands for something else. In other words, very little is what it seems to be on its surface.

(2) Dreams often display a radical discontinuity and shift between contexts, so that something which happened 20 years ago is just as real and significant as something which happened yesterday.

(3) On their surface, events are loosely joined, so that it takes time and work to figure out what connection, if any, there is between the disparate images that constitute the dream. As the great psychoanalysts have shown, it often takes a great deal of work and time between both analyst and patient to unravel the secrets of a dream. However, if the work and time are invested, then most dreams can be unraveled. And the unraveling reveals a deeper inner truth about the psyche of the dreamer than is available from the contents of everyday conscious life.

(4) The elements of a dream do not stand alone; they only exist and take on their meaning by virtue of all the other elements with which they are associated and the meaning of the entire dream itself.

(5) The final characteristic is that the entire dream revolves around the dreamer as both the prime participant and spectator in his or her own dream.

Music videos recreate nearly all of these dream characteristics. Their access, and hence the imagery they contain, is virtually unlimited. Videos are on nonstop for 24 hours a day. In the words of one analyst,[7] they are the very essence of continuous discontinuity or equally discontinuous continuity. The only way to understand them is to recognize them as short, prolonged bursts of sensual images.[8] That is, on their surface at least, they contain no apparent intellectual content.

The similarity of music videos to the structure of dreams is made further apparent in that one of their main goals is to remove history or ordinary time as we normally experience it so that the viewer can have the illusion of living forever. Indeed, the comparison with dreams is really not forced or overdrawn as soon as one appreciates that a great many music videos begin with someone either dreaming or daydreaming.[9]

Boundary Warping is revealed in other aspects as well which serve at the same time to reinforce even further the interpretation that the structure of dreams and the structure of music videos are nearly congruent. For instance, the gender of the performers in music videos is generally not fixed. Male and female figures often transform back and forth into one another so that the boundary between the sexes is extremely fluid if not virtually nonexistent. Even the boundaries between the various parts of the performers' bodies are not fixed as well. Both the bodies and the parts of the performers' personalities are at any instant capable of being broken apart into endless fragments each of which can have a separate existence of its own.

The unreality of music videos is apparent in other features as well. Grotesqueness is the norm, so that everything in the landscape—costumes, dress, and even colors—are all generally exaggerated.[10] But these exaggerations are nothing compared to the radical shifts and blurrings between images and contexts. The most incredible images are juxtaposed in time and space and often within the same space and time. At any one moment in time, one can see performers in luxuriant, unisex clothes, costumes, and fantasy scenes instantly interposed with the most pitiful looking, starving children. Thus, the pitifulness of the children is made even worse than anything we could have created if we had designed such horrible scenes from scratch.[11]

The dream motif is also seen in other elements as well. The characters are not only constantly transforming themselves so that even though they are unisexual they are still free to change back and forth between "male" unisexual creatures and "female" unisexual creatures. In addition, the figures are often menaced by grotesque appearing figures of "authority which serve to trigger powerful acts of destruction devoid of any moral or social context whatsoever."[12] Indeed, apocalypse is often a current theme.

Music videos not only invent their own world, but they invent the kind of uniqueness where it's a continual struggle to hold onto the boundaries of oneself.[13] Boundary Warping is thus not only a constant menace but it is in fact the central player in the drama. That is, the central player in music videos is strangely enough not the music itself. Finally, no discussion of music videos as a prime example of Boundary Warping would be complete without mention of the fact that music videos have successfully transgressed, and hence erased, the boundaries between commercials and shows. The commercials are the show. There is nothing else.

Music videos are indeed king in the land of Boundary Warping. They constitute a multiple warp and transgression between dreams, shows, commercials, sexuality, people, machines, and even the most pitiful scenes of suffering.

The Saturday Morning Kids' Shows

The most conspicuous aspect of the Saturday morning cartoon shows may well lie in the fact that the toy companies whose ads feature prominently are engaged in a process of the active creation of fantasy characters (archetypes) which are capable of literally taking on a life of their own. The discovery of archetypes by the Swiss psychologist Carl Jung, which we discuss in greater detail later in this book, is one of the most profound of the 20th century. Jung discovered that human experience was so deeply organized around recurrent symbols that they continually emerged in the dreams, fairy tales, and myths of the most widely scattered peoples over the face of the earth. These symbols which were the purest known to man Jung labeled archetypes, for example, the Evil Old Woman or Bad Mother, i.e., the Witch; the Strong Dominant Father or the King; the Young Prince; the idea of the Perfect Circle signifying Harmony and Completion in man; the sun as the supreme symbol for the Giver of Life; and so on.

What's distinctive about the Saturday morning kids' shows is that, unlike ancient fairy tales and myths where the central archetypes were located in a historical setting and story that was passed from generation to generation and was a deep part of the culture in which it was embedded, the archetypes that have been created by the toy manufacturers are detached from any broader social context for the sole purpose of selling products.[15] While this may not be Boundary Warping as we have referred to it earlier, it possesses nonetheless a number of disturbing features which thus qualify for inclusion under this general label.

One feature in particular more than justly qualifies under the heading of Boundary Warping. Hi-tech robots feature prominently in the Saturday morning kids' shows. Or rather half-human, half-hi-tech hybrid creatures often appear. What is both fascinating and disturbing at the same time is that the partnership between the parts is unequal. The hybrid form is not a marriage of equal parts, but instead on nearly every dimension, humans cede all power and abilities to their technological halves or counterparts.[14] Thus, the hi-tech robots or half-parts of the hybrid creatures usually possess greater power, ability, and intelligence. In effect, they are endowed with the ability to solve all human problems. In contrast, the humans are generally portrayed as helpless and usually crumble in the face of overwhelming problems.[15] Thus, humans are generally portrayed as both passive and paralyzed by their fears and limitations. Boundary Warping thus plays a prominent role in the universe in which such creatures exist because it is a world that you can never completely trust.[16] It is a world that is always on the verge of transforming instantly into something else.[17] The result is not only that the boundaries between humans and machines are blurred, but, even more significant, all boundaries are inherently unstable. There is no stability to existence whatsoever in such universes.

Music videos may be the undisputed winners in the Boundary Warp sweepstakes to date. They cross over more boundaries than any other currently available medium: dreams, waking, sex, people, machines, and commercials. But the victory is surely only temporary.

As with music videos, Boundary Warping also plays a prominent role in kids' TV because the programs are only thinly veiled disguises at best for program-length commercials. Once again, the barriers between ads and shows have been broken down. Only the formal distinction between shows and commercials remains and it's an increasingly small one at that. The distinction is in fact so small that thoughts which once would have been labeled as chilling and improbable are now highly improbable. What is there after all to prevent the enterprising manufacturer of literally any product from creating animated, talking versions of them that could be transmitted directly into viewers' homes? If the goal after all is to reach the young as much as possible everywhere, then why not go one step further and beam these new creations directly into the offices of pediatricians so that kids can view them while waiting for service? Indeed, why not send them everywhere, into shopping malls, playgrounds? Is any thought really too outrageous that it can be automatically ruled out from consideration?

The People's Court

The People's Court is generic brand, plain-wrap justice served up through the magic of TV.[18]

The whole format of *The People's Court* centers around ordinary people who are denied justice via traditional means or who want it speeded up. We are constantly reassured by the voice overrides of the announcer that while we are watching a TV program, everything is real because a real judge, although retired, presides. The presumed guarantor of the authenticity of the show consists of the endless repetition of the phrase "this is real; this is real; this is…"

The whole program is staged so that no one really loses. The awards and cost settlements are paid entirely by the show's producers (who then build these costs into syndication rights). The only real loss that accrues to both plaintiff and defendant is the potential humiliation of the loss of face on national TV. One might say in fact that humiliation serves as one of the deeper guarantors of the believability of the show. But to say even this is to miss a more important point.

The People's Court is to real justice as game shows are to reality. *The People's Court* is justice as a quiz show portrays it, with the judge as principal quizmaster. So, like TV news, the boundary between content, in this case justice, and entertainment is eroded once again.

Sorting the Serious From the Trivial

Boundary Warping ranges from the trivial and the frivolous to the socially significant and potentially earth-shattering. An example of the trivial is the discussion that has occurred in the late '80s concerning a new "art form," the "dramedy," i.e., a mixture of drama and the sitcom. It is perhaps a measure of the mindlessness of the TV networks and/or their insensitivity to the more serious forms of Boundary Warping that they would be more concerned about the erosion of the boundaries between drama and comedy than they are between entertainment and news. Clearly, some forms of Boundary Warping are more important than others. This only raises the critical question as to how one differentiates between them.

First of all, we need to make clear that we are not opposed to Boundary Warping per se. The complete elimination of Boundary Warping is neither possible nor desirable. More importantly, essential elements of Boundary Warping are fundamentally present in what we humans call reality.

Ever since the noted German philosopher Immanuel Kant, educated people have realized that both the experiencing of reality as well as its description are much more dependent on the structure of our minds than naive realists would have us believe. As a result, what we call and experience as reality is extremely malleable. It is dependent in part on our needs and purposes. Contrary to the common notion that reality is "something out there" uninfluenced by human hands and minds, we humans contribute a great deal of our nature to what we experience as reality in the first place and how we describe it in the second.

One of the best ways to see this is to consider the analogy of the human mind as a computer. This way of looking at the mind is so powerful that we are convinced that were he alive today, Kant himself would have used the analogy of the human mind as a computer as a vivid way to demonstrate his theory of human knowledge.

Computers are very carefully designed to accept inputs from the outside world that are only of a certain kind. The things that are fed into a computer must be of the right form or the computer will not be able to recognize them in the first place. Most computers accept either electrical signals or punched cards. In the case of electrical signals, magnetized tapes are used in order to get them into a computer. As for punched cards, holes are either punched in cards or left filled in. In both cases, the effect is that the computer is able to read input data as a series of "ones" (if a "one" is present then a portion of a tape will be magnetized or a punched hole will be made in a card) or "zeros" (in the case of a magnetic tape, a portion of the tape will not be magnetized or in the case of a punched card, the hole will be left filled in). The point is that computers are very carefully constructed to receive only a certain kind of input data, ones or zeros, that are imprinted on valid media, tapes or cards carefully manufactured to be of certain sizes. These in turn must be input into the correct receiving mechanism attached to the computer.

One could literally throw cards or tapes representing hard data from the external world at a computer all day long but unless the computer were designed and built in such a way to accept tapes or cards, that is, unless it had the right kind of hardware to read incoming tapes or cards, the computer would not be able to have experience of the outside world in the form of zeros or ones. Further, if not for the software (internal programs) stored in it, capable of making sense of zeros and ones, the computer would never be able to recognize patterns in the stream of zeros and ones and hence reach conclusions about the nature of the outside world. Thus, at least two things are needed to have experience: an ability (1) to input, i.e., receive data from the outside world, and once in, (2) to make sense of what it has received. Neither of these two critical abilities is a property of external things themselves. They are properties of the computer and by analogy our minds. The structure of our minds thus plays a fundamental role in: (1) what we experience as reality, (2) how we experience it, (3) what we characterize as reality, and (4) how we characterize it.

The pattern recognition routines as well as the input mechanisms of computers do not determine the *content* of the input, but they do prescribe its *form*. That is, computers themselves do not determine the patterns of zeros and ones that are fed into them but they do set up a constraint on what is fed in. The patterns that are fed in supposedly encompass data descriptive of some problem in the outside world; for example, the incidence of various crimes in a certain neighborhood, the amount of air pollution over a city, and so forth. Data not input in this form cannot be recognized by the computer.

Consider another even simpler example. Imagine the existence of a highly intelligent wine glass, i.e., one with a mind that was able to ask questions. Suppose such a wine glass asked, "How is it that no matter what the quality, bouquet, or the origin of the wine that is poured into me, it always has the same shape? How is this possible?" If our wine glass were intelligent enough, it would come to the realization that *it* supplied some critical feature of its experience of the wine that was poured into it, namely, its shape. Everything else that was characteristic of the wine, its flavor, color, bouquet, country of origin, was supplied by something or someone else external to the wine glass. None of these things were determined by the wine glass.

The point of both these examples is that in order for human beings to have experience or to gain knowledge about the world, there must be something built into their minds that is capable of receiving data or facts characteristic of the outside world or reality itself. The computer is not able to get in certain facts in the form of zeros and ones about the outside world unless the data are input in the right form. Similarly, the wine glass is not able to get in data in the form of wine from the outside world unless it is made in a certain kind of shape so that it can contain the wine.

Knowledge about the world is the result of an interaction between both the structure of the computer and that of the data that can be input into it, between the shape of the wine glass and the fluidity of the wine. Both the computer and the wine glass supply a critical, crucial ingredient to both the structure of reality as well as to our knowledge about it. The wine glass does not create the external reality that is fed into it, i.e., the wine; it merely possesses a shape whereby wine can be stored in it. Likewise, computers do not create what is on the cards or the tapes that are fed into them, and in this sense they do not create the outside world, but they do possess a set of internal *categories* so that whatever external reality is fed into them can be pigeonholed.

In the case of computers, these categories are in the form of "addresses." They work much like mailboxes along a street. They tell a computer where to put the series of zeros and ones that are punched on cards or tapes. For instance, computers are typically built to read the separate columns on cards and to place the zeros and ones in each separate column in a distinct mailbox or address inside the computer's memory. Once all the data from the cards are inside the computer, the computer's internal programs take over. The computer in essence may be programmed to add the zeros and ones on all the odd (or even) mailboxes together.

What has all this to do with Boundary Warping? Our minds are not only built in such a manner so that we can experience reality, but so that we can experience unreality as well. Both arise from underlying needs as well as certain abilities of our minds. For instance, the ability to recognize the human face is one of the earliest and most fundamental that man possesses. It obviously serves human survival well given the long and intense dependence human infants have on their parents. It also allows us to bond with others and therefore move human relations to a deeper plane beyond mere survival. But the ability to recognize the human face also means that we have the ability to distort it if need be in order to serve deeper needs. Thus, in the early days of magazine advertising in the '20s and '30s, advertisers discovered that women were predisposed towards printed images that portrayed them as elegant beings in contrast to the mundane inelegant lives that most led. Elegance itself was conveyed through drawings that literally elongated the bodies and faces of women to pencil thin proportions. Our minds are thus not only built to represent reality "as it is" but also to represent or distort reality as we'd "like it to be."

The drawing of boundaries is one of the principal ways in which we give order to our world. When traditional boundaries are threatened or dissolved suddenly, we experience disorientation, often severe. For example, a few years ago a group of artists designed a "space bridge" between Los Angeles and New York. Two windows in major department stores, one in New York and one in Los Angeles, were converted into giant TV screens. Each TV screen projected images from the opposite city. The effect was as if one were looking through a window a continent away. Word quickly spread and people began to congregate at convenient points in time so that they could see friends and relatives on both coasts. There was some mild disorientation given the differences between the time zones so that when it was dark in New York it was still light in L.A. and vice versa, but people rapidly learned to adjust. In this way, the time zones or geographical boundaries between both coasts were dissolved somewhat.

Another example shows even more clearly what happens when traditional boundaries are collapsed or blurred more drastically. The same group of artists performed an experiment that involved the merging of images of male and female dancers on a TV screen. A male dancer performed in one room; a female, in another. Thus, the physical locations of the dancers were separate. At a certain time, both dancers began to dance free form. A TV camera in each room shot a separate picture of each dancer, but only a joint, superimposed image was fed back on a TV screen in each room to both dancers. It not only took time for the dancers to coordinate their separate images or movements to get in sync with one another, but it took even more time for them to feel comfortable when their images began to overlap or penetrate one another. The dancers not only learned to coordinate their dance movements but the degree to which their images could penetrate one another. At first, the dancers literally experienced anxiety as their body images invaded one another. They experienced discomfort as the normal boundaries of their bodies were no longer intact. The dancers behaved as though not merely their body images were invading one another but that the actual sex of the other person was penetrating their bodies.

We are programmed and conditioned to maintain boundaries. The trouble is that we live in a time when more boundaries than ever before are either suspect or under attack. For instance, as we alluded to earlier in this chapter, the boundaries between professions and academic disciplines are more suspect than ever. The boundaries between the sexes are no longer clear-cut or as well established as they once were. We have unisex clothing, unisex hairstyles, and even unisex speech. Traditional age differences are no longer as sacrosanct as they once were. It is common to find children acting and dressing as adults and adults acting and dressing as children.

While the burden or blame for this cannot be placed solely on TV, there is no question that the media must shoulder a great deal of responsibility. Joshua Meyrowitz[19] has developed an important theory that explains parts of a phenomenon of Boundary Warping even though he did not call it such.

Meyrowitz takes off from the work of Marshall McLuhan and Erving Goffman. Goffman was surely one of the most influential sociologists who has ever lived. One of his most important books was *The Presentation of Self in Everyday Life.* Goffman's thesis was that much of human behavior could be understood from the perspective of life as a stage upon which we play. Certain portions of life were played on stage in front of the audience while others were acted out backstage hidden from view. The up front portions of life were those situations where we performed our roles as husband, wife, father, mother, teacher, student, judge, etc., in front of others. The backstage portions were those private occasions and spaces where we let down our hair, dropped our formal roles, and talked candidly to our intimate friends, associates, and colleagues about the problems of our professions, our lives, what we thought about those in front of whom we had to act.

One of the critical points about TV, and increasingly of all media today, is that there is little backstage behavior that is private any longer. In effect, there is no backstage anymore. Everyone seemingly confesses everything on TV, from pending divorces to current infidelities. We have no need for secrets anymore. In the entertainment society, everything is confessional, public, out front.

Through watching TV, children are able to observe things that adults have traditionally done and thought about in private. Through TV, children can observe both staged and "real" versions of adult lives: sex, finance, improprieties, etc. (Thus, John Tower confesses infidelities and promises sobriety at the public confessional of our age, TV.) Television brings the lives of the rich and famous as well as the poor into everyone's home. It brings war directly into our living rooms. It's the great leveler. While TV is thus not solely responsible for the dissolution of traditional boundaries, it is nonetheless one of the most powerful forces behind it.

Human culture is both the reflection of and an extension of our minds. The various professions, for instance, have fought to put special boundaries around the realms of experience or expertise they treat. In terms of the computer analogy we used earlier, the various professions in effect have different computers. They take in different inputs and process them differently. In terms of the wine glass analogy, the professions not only pour or cast their problems into different wine glasses but also take in altogether different wines to begin with. In other words, the various professions treat the "same" problems differently as well as focus on or take in different problems to begin with. In effect, the boundaries between professions are the differences between the categories they use to structure the problems they treat. Thus, for instance, the medical profession's diagnosis of our nation's drug problem is in general very different from the legal profession's. One wants to treat drug abuse as an "illness," the other as a "crime." The difficulty is that drug abuse is both and much more besides.

What has become increasingly clearer over the course of this century is that the traditional boundaries between the professions are less and less suited to dealing with the complex reality with which we are faced. The primary purposes of the professions are to solve human problems. Thus, each of the professions represented in Figure 1 exists primarily to help solve human problems. What has become clearer is that as reality itself has become more complex, the traditional boundaries between professions inhibits the solving of critical human problems. As the complexity of reality itself jumps over more and more traditional boundaries—geopolitical, time zones, organizations—we need to reexamine and *dis*solve many, if not most, of the borders between professions in order to deal more cogently with reality.

At the same time, in reaction to this complexity, we witness more and more the illegitimate crossing of boundaries between industries, e.g., most prominently between entertainment and the news (see Figure 1). (Each circle in Figure 1 represents a different level of social reality. Thus, for instance, the legal system is broader than the legal profession, since the legal system not only encompasses law schools and the American Bar Association but also the courts and the penal system. The circles intersect since there are obvious points of overlap between where the professions, systems, and industries and individual issues all come into contact.) This is how we differentiate the

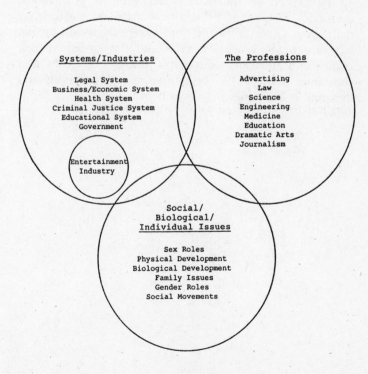

Figure 1.

legitimate from the illegitimate crossing of boundaries. In a word, we have much less fear and concern of the crossing of boundaries *between professions* than we have of the crossing of the boundaries *between professions and industries*.

The boundaries between professions impede problem solving while the dissolution of other boundaries diverts us from attacking critical problems. The primary purpose of news is not to entertain but to inform. To accomplish this does not mean that news should be dull or boring but only that entertainment is merely a handservant of the news, not its master. The critical issue is that of primary intent. When entertainment becomes the master ruling the house of any one of the professions, then we doubt seriously that any society that sanctions this can endure for long.

The most interesting problems in human culture have always existed on the borders between the professions, industries, systems, and the critical areas which affect our daily lives. Entertainment, and increasingly all media, trivialize these boundaries. As a result, the border between reality and unreality which has always been thin and constantly shifting has become even more fragile and dynamic in our times than ever before.

4. Manufacturing People
The Prosthetic Society

At an otherwise pleasant dinner party he attended the other evening, Dabney Coleman made a nice woman cry.

"I was doing my stuff, my sarcastic thing, and she didn't know I was kidding," Coleman confesses. "I thought she would get it, and she didn't."

Lauded for his talent at portraying characters that have been called everything from smarmy to sleazy to just plain mean...Coleman admits that over the years, *the blacker side of these roles have crept into his personality* [italics ours].

"I like playing those sarcastic characters, and I like doing it in my private life too, as a joke," Coleman says. "It's now become a part of my social humor."

—Steve Weinstein, "They Deliver the Slaps," *Los Angeles Times*, Nov. 11, 1987, p. 1

Television has gone tabloid. The seamy underside of life is being bared in a new rash of true-crime series and contrived-confrontation talk shows. They are cheap to make—$25,000 to $50,000 an episode, one-tenth the average cost of an episode for a network series. And the shows rake in big profits.

For years, television operated on the premise that the biggest audiences are lured with the least objectionable programs. Nowadays, that formula doesn't seem to work as well as it once did. The videoscape is increasingly cluttered. Some 500 game shows, talk shows, and series reruns compete for the fragmented attention of television viewers.

The new shows rise above the crowd by focusing on the sleazy, the sordid, and the downbeat. *Re-enactments of actual crimes are popular, and, even more perverse, the shows sometimes ask real-life victims to play themselves in the drama*... [italics ours].

Coming soon: A series that features actual murder trials, a series on missing children, and, yes, even more shows with dramatic re-enactments of real crimes....

But the new wave is even more outrageous than ever before. Television producers are discovering that fictional violence isn't enough for viewers anymore. "People are jaded by the predominance of crime fiction," says Michael L. Linder, the executive producer of "America's Most Wanted."

In a recent special with Geraldo Rivera as host, "Murder: Live From Death Row," 30 million viewers saw footage of an actual murder of a convenience store customer. The producers used the videotape from the store's security cameras. Mr. Rivera interviewed several convicted murderers about their crimes, encouraging them to share the grisly details. The highlight of the show: a prison interview with mass murderer Charles Manson.

—Dennis Kneale, "Titillating Channels, TV Is Going Tabloid As Shows Seek Sleaze and Find Profits, Too—Programs Focus on True Tales of Terror and Misfortune; Low Cost, High Ratings—Did It All Begin With Oprah?" *The Wall Street Journal*, May 18, 1988, pp. 1, 18.

At the height of the Irangate hearings in 1988 over the illegal disbursement of funds to the Nicaragua Contras, Fawn Hall, Colonel Oliver North's secretary, became something of a celebrity. Her loyalty to her embattled boss, her general demeanor and the way she conducted herself during the hearings, her strikingly good looks, her overall association with North who was deemed a hero of sorts by a certain segment of the American public—all these factors and more contributed to Fawn's newfound status in the public eye. Fawn's star had in fact risen so fast and had shone so brightly that there was even "'serious' Hollywood talk" (an oxymoron if ever there was) of Farrah Fawcett playing Fawn in the miniseries devoted to the controversy. The judgment was that Fawn was not quite ready to play herself on screen since she wasn't yet a big enough celebrity. She was, however, judged promising enough to be signed by the powerful William Morris Agency.

To build up her celebrity status over time, plans were laid to have Fawn make appearances on various soap operas. She was judged enough of a celebrity to start making appearances with other celebrities. The seeds were thus sown for the eventuality of Fawn and Farrah appearing together, thus completing another of TV's magic circles: The joint presence of Farrah (Fawn's simulated stand-in and an acknowledged celebrity in her own right) and her simulatee (Fawn, a recently-made celebrity).

Since the consumption of celebrities is so great in modern societies, especially in our own, their freshness or shelf life is extremely short. As a result, celebrities have to be produced at a faster and faster rate in order to satisfy public demand. The consequence is that by the time this or any other book has been published the names of Fawn and Ollie may have long faded from memory. The "15 minutes in the limelight of fame" that will be due all of us, according to artist Andy Warhol, will have long since passed by both Fawn and Ollie.

While celebrities may come and go at a faster and faster rate, fortunately the principles which govern their interactions are more enduring. Even though Farrah and Fawn may pass speedily from the scene only to reemerge in a hundred other forms, the principles involved in their specific case illustrate a number of important things about celebrities in particular and unreality in general.

Once one has achieved a certain status, then all visual renditions, incarnations, and images of a celebrity are "equal" in a certain sense. A "live" TV appearance, a cartoon, a caricature, an electronic image, an animation, and a flashback are all equal on TV. To be clear, we are not contending that all images on all media in all settings are equal. Obviously, standing next to the "real, live" Farrah is pretty high on the pole of celebrity experience. Also, we are not saying that all celebrities themselves are equal in stature. Some are clearly higher and more powerful than others.

What we are saying is that on TV in particular, and increasingly in all media, all renderings of a celebrity are free to coexist and to interact simultaneously with one another. In this special sense, all images are equal and nearly all command the same attention and weight and are thus equally worthy of appearing together. For example, a TV special starring Farrah, or any other celebrity, is free in principle to feature the "real, live" Farrah along with male or female impersonators, animated cartoon characters, electronic images, look alikes, characters she has either played in the past or she is planning to play in the future. Thus, the critical point about Fawn and Farrah is *not* that one, Fawn, represents "reality" and the other, Farrah, represents "unreality," but that *both are images* and as such are simultaneously a mixture of reality and unreality of unknown, and perhaps unknowable, proportions.

The new media represent the ultimate in the democratization of images. They are the latest inheritors of a long historical trend. Prior to the invention of photography in the 19th century, only the rich and/or famous could afford to have their portraits painted and thus be immortalized for posterity. The invention of the camera and the widespread diffusion of photography radically changed this. In principle, even the poorest now had access to immortality. Further, the ordinary citizen had available to him or her in a short period of time a greater number of portraits than the wealthy could have accumulated over an entire lifetime.

Contemporary media are thus only the latest in a long, continuous line in the democratization of images. It does not follow, however, that because all incarnations, images, or forms of rendering are increasingly equal in all media in modern society that the means of producing images are themselves equal. The final end products may be treated the same or produce the same effects on audiences but the different means of producing images are not the same and do not produce the same general consequences. It is important to appreciate this in order to have a deeper understanding of the different forms of unreality and of the other mechanisms for producing unreality beyond Boundary Warping which we explored in the last chapter.

The fact that increasingly all images are equal is itself illustrative of another facet of Boundary Warping. However, the democratization of images is also illustrative of another of the major mechanisms for producing unreality: Image or People Engineering. As we mentioned in the last chapter, all of the major mechanisms for creating unreality overlap greatly with one another. This is not just because the phenomenon of unreality is itself complex, but as the quotes from the *Wall Street Journal* at the beginning of this chapter illustrate, it is in the direct interest of the various media to mix different levels and kinds of unreality in order to win audiences.

As we pointed out in the last chapter, to differentiate between reality and unreality, it is necessary to have at least two critical faculties: the ability to be able to differentiate in the first place, and the desire to exercise the powers of discrimination in the second place. The ability to differentiate, the values to appreciate the differences, and the desire to exercise them are like any other human skills or talents. They must be constantly exercised or they vanish over time.

One of the most frightening aspects of unreality is that increasingly it is less and less in the interest of the media that we be able to differentiate between reality and unreality. To the contrary, it is to the advantage of the media that we be increasingly unable or unwilling to differentiate. Reason: the indiscriminate mixing of various levels and kinds of reality and unreality sells TV programs, books, tabloid and magazine articles, products, political candidates, etc., on an unparalleled scale. It is in the self interest of various groups that we neither care nor are able to differentiate.

The growing inability to differentiate as well as our decreased desire to be able to do so would be of little consequence were it not for the fact that *we are literally on the threshold of being able to design and to manufacture people to present specifications at every conceivable level of human existence.* This is precisely what differentiates our age from earlier periods. No one, certainly not us, can contend that earlier eras were any better or morally superior to ours when it comes to inventing unreality. One can in fact contend that earlier eras pursued unreality with a vengeance that would rival ours. The critical difference is that *earlier ages did not possess the technology to create as many different forms of unreality, the means to distribute it as widely, as well as the technology to intrude as deeply as we can into every aspect of human existence.*

Currently, we will soon be able to intervene at the surface or cosmetic levels of existence, the mental or psychological, the physiological, the molecular, and even the genetic. The depths to which we can now actively intervene or manufacture people makes the ability to discriminate between the real and the unreal of increased importance. At the same time, perhaps because of or in reaction to this newfound ability, we seem less concerned to differentiate.

Order Out of Disorder: The Varieties of Manufacturing People

One of the most interesting things about complex phenomena is that if you stick with them long enough, they reveal an order that underlies them. Further, it is always an order which is somewhat unexpected. It is no different with unreality.

The situation may be similar to the phenomenon of chaos, the subject of a new science that has been created over the last 30 years.[1] If we take the output, for example, electrical signals, of certain very simple systems (e.g., physical processes which are easy to describe mathematically) and then feed the output back in as the next round of input to the system, and repeat this whole process hundreds and even thousands of times, after thousands of cycles the output for certain systems converges towards a very specific value that represents a stable end-state of the system. However, if we change some of the critical dimensions of the system by an exceedingly small amount, the output after the thousandth cycle of the same system can bear no relationship at all to the output at the end of the thousandth and first cycle, and so on for every succeeding cycle. In other words, for certain configurations of even very simple systems, the output from cycle to cycle can vary unpredictably. The system's behavior, in short, can become chaotic: impossible to describe, predict, or control. Even more bewildering, if one keeps changing certain critical dimensions or features of the system, the system's behavior can become calm or smooth again. Keep changing the system further and it can enter zones of chaos again. In fact, bands or zones of chaos and smoothness can crowd or pile up against one another, and in this sense, one can speak of bands of order within disorder and vice versa.

How? Why? No one knows for sure, but we do know that for certain systems, exceedingly small initial differences in the nature of the system can produce exceedingly large differences in its final output. For instance, it is not difficult to write down the equations that govern weather conditions on our planet. And in fact one of the reasons why computers were first invented was to perform the large number of calculations necessary in order to solve these equations so that one could make accurate weather predictions. What was not anticipated was that exceedingly small, if not trivial, differences in the initial output into the equations (for example, data representing initial weather conditions at a particular point in time) produced dramatically large differences in their output (i.e., predictions as to what the weather would be five days later). The result is that the forecasting of weather by computers was deemed impossible. The equations are so sensitive to initial conditions that even if the whole planet were split up into one-foot squares and conditions at each corner of each square were fed into the weather equations, unknown differences as to what was happening in the middle of each square would be enough to throw off the whole process of weather prediction. This extreme sensitivity is called The Butterfly Effect; i.e., a butterfly flapping its wings in the middle of each square would be enough to throw off the whole weather prediction effort.

The major break in weather forecasting came only when we got away from the equations and were able to place satellites high above the earth in stationary orbits to produce pictures of weather patterns hours away. Only then could one make predictions based upon pictures of the phenomena and not on mathematical models or equations of it.

Of course, chaos and unreality are not equivalent phenomena. There is an underlying order, however, that explains those aspects of unreality which involve the manufacturing of people or what we have called Image or People Engineering. In fact, we believe that the major forms of manufacturing people are clear enough so that we can lay them out in a table.

Table 1 identifies six major ways by which we are currently able to manufacture people. Each row of the table captures a different means of manufacturing. As one moves across each row, the different columns identify a different level of intensity or depth to which the manufacturing process intrudes into a person's existence. Thus, column 1 or "Suppression" identifies the lowest level of intrusion while column 5 or "Creation" identifies the highest or deepest level of intrusion.

Since the table appears complex at first, we're going to proceed through it in stages. We're going to start with a brief discussion of soap operas as a particular type of unreality (row 1). By the end of the discussion, the relation of soaps to the table will be clear.

Soaps, The Mythic Past

Like the personalities of TV newscasters which provide the only lasting link of continuity in a world of extremely fluctuating events, Soaps serve pretty much the same

TABLE 1
MEANS AND EXTENT OF REALITY ALTERATION

Means of Alteration/ Distortion	Extent/Depth of Alteration/Distortion			
	Suppression 1	Mild/Moderate: Enhancement 2	Misrepresentation 3	Severe/Total: Replacement/Creation 4 5
1. Theatrical	Absence of Social Problems	Soap Operas: Traditional Feminine Values	Mythic Communities	Fictive Indentification: Loss of One's Character/Personality Extreme Identification, Internalization
2. Surface/ Cosmetic	Dress, Voice Training, Makeovers, Coaching	Facelifts	Image Creation	Total Body Makeover
3. Psycho-logical	Conscious Control, Gaming	Acting	Role Playing, Conning	Brainwashing; Deep Internalization, Personality Replacement, Complete Merging/Identification With The Role
4. Medical/ Prosthetic	Drugs	Steroids	Prosthesis	Deep Transplantation, Genetic Alteration, Deep Fusion
5. Indus-trial/ Social/	Traditional Celebrity Production: Pre-Organized Industry		PR, Organized Celebrity Manufacturing	Sociopathic Organization: Jonestown
6. Elec-tronic/ Techno-logical	Reduction	"Real Characters" Enlargement	Misportrayal	Creation of Archetypes/Nonexistent Characters Electronic Characters (Max Headroom, Electronic Landscapes

function only in an even more personal sense.[2] Some Soap communities have been around for over 30 years. As a result, they allow the viewer an outlet in which to make prolonged social contact in a society that is governed increasingly by severe disruption and disarray. At a minimum, Soaps provide a reprieve, however mild, from the loneliness that is widespread in contemporary America.

Soaps of course do much more than this. They are not just an outlet for loneliness, but are among the safest of outlets for vicarious identification. One can get caught up daily with other people without having to really get involved, i.e., do anything with the characters that would entail real risks. One can invite in daily to one's home strangers who are not really strangers because one knows them in many cases better than one knows one's own friends, neighbors, and even relatives. There is no danger because the characters make no real life demands.[3]

What's interesting is that no matter what particular property one states about Soaps, or any other particular form of unreality, there is always another property lurking beneath the surface that reveals an additional basis for their widespread and never ending appeal. For instance, the men on Soaps generally display a far greater degree of interpersonal competency and intimacy than most men are capable of. Soaps thus fulfill the important function of providing women in particular with the illusion of intimacy, an intimacy that they generally cannot obtain from their spouses because it is missing basically from their emotional repertoire. The most acute observations about Soaps may well be that "in daytime TV both men and women are judged by women's values,"[4] i.e., interpersonal intimacy and competency that does not revolve around commercial success. To put it succinctly, "Only on Soaps do men value the verbal intimacy lacking in most marriages."[5] Thus, true to form, Soaps enhance certain properties of people (feminine values) and suppress others (masculine) and completely misrepresent others (the relative absence of social problems).

It is of course no surprise that Soaps recreate amazingly well a mythic view of America's golden past. Amid rapid, if not cataclysmic, social change, Soaps paint an idealized vision of America's small town past. The critical thing that must be noted is that the past that Soaps create is a manufactured illusion. They are a creation in the truest sense of the word, i.e., they are not fundamentally a recreation of America's past. The difference is important since it accounts for why we have placed Soaps under the general mechanism of Image or People Engineering.

Soaps are completely manufactured creations because not only do they invent people, particularly males, whose emotional sensitivities are way beyond the norm found in most societies, but they also establish a social context that is highly artificial. For example, there is never any institutionalized racism on Soaps. For another, the Equal Rights Amendment or ERA doesn't exist; it never happened.[6] In other words, all problems are completely individual and personal. They are not due to any forces locked deeply within the political or social structure of society.

The reasons for this are not hard to understand. TV is extremely adept at presenting individual dilemmas. In the words of Norman Lear, "TV loves moist," e.g., unfettered and extravagant displays of emotion. This is because commercial TV is a medium which has been especially adapted to the capturing of and focusing on emotions to the almost extreme exclusion of ideas. Unlike print media, which have to describe emotions and feeling, TV can let one actually see them; i.e., one can see the nuances of facial expression which are so revealing of inner character. Little wonder then why TV in particular has become a medium devoted almost exclusively to the visual display of emotions.

If all problems are personal and hence not part of either the political or social structure of society, then it follows that all problems are cured ultimately through individual therapeutic means or personal self-insight, not through the fundamental restructuring of business, political, and social institutions. Thus, on most Soaps therapeutic intervention generally replaces religious intervention. As a number of observers have noted, the religious society has been replaced by the therapeutic one.[7]

As we shall see later when we examine some of the roots of our culture that have led to the latest hyper craze for unreality, America has always had deep yearnings and strivings for therapeutic redemption.[8] And Soaps are only the latest manifestation and currently the most easily available form in a long line of therapeutic aids.

The function of such aids has remained pretty much the same: to provide psychological relief from the stresses generated by a bureaucratic, technological society that often demeans and dehumanizes its members who are locked in its grips. This in fact probably constitutes the deepest appeal of unreality, i.e., to free us psychologically from the overbearing demands of a harsh complicated reality. In this context, *there is nothing absolutely wrong with a "modicum or moderate" amount of unreality. Taken in moderate, controlled doses, unreality can even be beneficial to prolonged social life*—much as aspirin in moderate doses is helpful in warding off heart attacks. *Unreality in the form of Boundary Warping can even be a boon to creativity by freeing us from outmoded and constricted boxes.* Taken in overdoses, however, as a daily diet—with little or no awareness of what one is consuming—unreality can be as fatal to the social spirit, imagination, and consciousness of a people as overdoses of cocaine can be to the physical body of society. This point will become critical in a moment when we discuss some of the more dangerous aspects of Soaps.

Row 1 in Table 1 summarizes our discussion thus far. The lowest level of unreality as listed under column 1 is the general absence or suppression of social problems on Soaps. Column 2 stresses that soaps generally emphasize traditional or stereotypical feminine values, i.e., the men who appear on Soaps have *enhanced* emotional repertoires. Column 3, on the other hand, summarizes the fact that Soaps generally misrepresent, i.e., mythologize, the nature of past communities.

Columns 4 and 5 touch on a whole new class or type of mental illness that has been associated recently with Soaps in particular and the phenomenon of celebrityhood in general.[9] The phenomenon of Soaps becomes especially disturbing when the degree of identification with their characters becomes so intense that it substitutes either in part or in toto for the personalities of viewers.

Societies everywhere have always produced people whose personalities and identities were either weakly or incompletely formed. Heroes, celebrities, royalty, historical personages have always served as living substitutes for the deficient parts of the personalities of people whose own personalities were weak or insufficiently formed. What's alarming is that modern societies provide an ever abundant, ever increasing supply of fictive personalities with whom weak or incomplete people can identify or compensate for their own deficient personalities.[10]

The worst, most extreme, form of identification occurs when, for instance, a Mark Chapman identifies so closely with a John Lennon that he projects unwanted or undesirable aspects of himself on to Lennon. When the unwanted projections are so powerful and so bad that the person can not accept them as characteristic of himself/herself, then often the only way to get rid of the projections is to kill the person, in this case John Lennon, who has been chosen as the unconscious embodiment of them. To put it mildly, this is Boundary Warping of the most extreme and most dangerous form. One is not able to keep straight—literally—the boundaries between himself/herself and some other, typically famous or well known person.

Other forms of Boundary Warping can be just as dangerous. Because of their weak identity, some people don't just "watch" a soap opera. They literally become a part of it. In effect there is no boundary between them and the drama. Of course, there is often an amusing side to all this. Some of the letters that are written to the producers of Soaps inquire as to how to contact a particular character or where a particular character was raised. The persons who write such letters are unable to accept that the characters are purely fictional. After all, they are real or they wouldn't be on TV. This stops becoming a laughing matter when the crossover is so great that the person literally becomes either the character he or she is witnessing or needs the character in order to live.

If Soaps generally fulfill this function for individual

weak personalities, then why shouldn't unreality as a general phenomenon provide an equivalent function for society as a whole? Doesn't unreality after all fill up our increasingly incomprehensible, unfulfilling lives?

Medicine: The Living Intrusion

We're going to skip discussion of some of the remaining rows in Table 1, not because they are unimportant or completely self explanatory, but to the contrary are so important that they are deserving of an extended treatment of their own which we take up in the next chapter. To a certain extent, rows 2 and 3, surface/cosmetic and psychological, are somewhat self explanatory. More important, they are really subparts of row 5.

As we have been contending all along, one of the most important reasons why unreality has become so powerful a force in our times is that it has become institutionalized on a wide scale. It is the basis of a new industry that for the most part is hidden from direct view. The end result is that the production of unreality is not only organized in our society but it is a multi-billion-dollar-a-year industry. Indeed, unreality is so much a part of our society that it is not even possible to determine precisely just how much money is spent on it. It plays the role of oxygen; it's everywhere and nowhere at the same time. As a result, all the rows of Table 1 are really subparts of row 5 in that all the mechanisms serve an industry. The industrial side of unreality is thus so important that we have chosen to make it the subject of the next chapter.

Before leaving this chapter, we wish, however, to discuss two remaining rows of Table 1: Medical/Prosthetic and Electronic/Technological. The extreme right-hand column of row 4 shows what a highly advanced technological society is capable of. By now, most people are vaguely aware of the revolution that is occurring in genetic engineering even if they don't fully comprehend it. They know that it has something to do with producing bigger, smarter mice and growing bigger, richer tomatoes and so on. What they don't appreciate is that the medical revolution hits much closer to home. One doesn't have to go to the arcane level of genetics or molecules to appreciate the impacts of this new revolution.

For example, researchers at the University of Texas recently announced the invention of a new kind of synthetic bone material. The revolutionary new material is not only lighter and stronger than the old kinds that were used to make repairs, but in addition possesses a property that older materials never did. The new synthetic material is not only more compatible with living tissue, but indeed so much so that it is the only known material thus far into which blood vessels can grow. In effect, blood vessels are capable of converting what was previously inert material into new living material:

> Scientists at the University of Texas have developed a new type of synthetic bone that is virtually identical to natural bone. The new material is much stronger than previous bone substitutes and better able to withstand stress, the Texas researchers said Tuesday.
>
> Tests have shown that once the new material is implanted in animals, it is slowly broken down by bodily processes and replaced by living bone. This stimulation of new bone growth suggests that grafts should last indefinitely, the researchers said.
>
> When they implant the porous material in animals...the animal's own natural bone covers and grows into the pores over a two-to-four week period and blood vessels grow into the pores. Over longer periods of time, the synthetic bone is broken down by specialized cells and replaced with natural bone—just as the body's own bone is continually replaced. "This is the only material I know of that, if you put it in the body, capillaries vasculate, cells grow...and real bone replaces it," said MIT's Alan Davidson.[11]

One wonders whether human beings are on the verge of becoming like modern cars. In effect, the only thing that is still American about many cars is their nameplate. The actual car itself may be composed of more foreign than American parts. Is the same thing now happening to humans? What after all is the dividing line between inert and living material? What is dead? What is alive? What is real? These are no longer academic questions. They are certainly no longer questions for which there are available obvious or easy answers.

Electronic Worlds

It is the link with modern computers that has made TV capable of creating virtually any image that can be thought of and described. The increasingly sophisticated graphics packages that are now widely available to the users of home computers enables virtually anyone to create his/her own universe according to his/her own specs.[12] Thus, weird physical objects that do not obey the usual laws of physics can be created as well as the weirdest imaginable creatures.

The most significant, if not ominous, long run impact of these new capabilities lies in the fact that we are getting closer day by day to the point where electronic images of "real" people can be stored within a computer. Furthermore, such images are getting ever closer to our ability to program them to interact with other images which are either stored or live.[13] Thus, the other images with which any image can interact can be either real, live, or other previous simulations of the initial person or thing, in short, whatever one is capable of putting into a computer. The fundamental rationale for all of this is not to allow engineering nerds to play with highly sophisticated electronic toys. No, the real reason is that the networks, the electronic and computer manufacturers, the ad agencies, and even the big toy companies, all have poured considerable monies into the development of Image Engineering. This is because it allows all of the interested parties to achieve and to maintain a degree of control over electronic images that they cannot achieve and maintain over live human subjects.[14]

Consider all of the things that one can do with electronic images. Note further that the list is only partial; it is growing every day; and finally, ask the question, how many of these things can one do with real, live human subjects? Electronic images can be: (1) *idealized* to preset specs, (2) *distorted* to preset specs, (3) *recreated* at any time in any place, (4) *reproduced*, (5) *enhanced*, (6) *improved*, (7) *isolated*, (8) *coexistent* with any other image, live, real, or simulated, (9) *saved indefinitely*, i.e., as opposed to humans, they have a near infinite shelf life, (10) *fragmented* or split, i.e., the individual parts of an image—an eye or an ear—can take on a life or a personality of its own, (11) *enlarged* or conversely *reduced* grossly in size, (12) *given multiple and bizarre colors*, and on, and on.

A simple example is that of a live image of a baseball player. A TV picture can be taken of him making a spectacular catch or hitting a home run. It can then be played back as an "instant rerun," or it can be frozen for "stop action." One can "zoom in" on any part or feature to examine or to highlight. The image can be stored or saved electronically for later editing in terms of any one of the characteristics noted above. By these means, one can thus frame a commercial which shows the ballplayer looking at himself making the spectacular catch or hitting the spectacular hit, all the while touting the benefits of some product. The combinations are thus virtually endless. Is there any wonder then why a technology-oriented society such as ours wouldn't seize upon such means? Why settle for entertaining or amusing ourselves as Neil Postman[15] has proposed when we literally have it within our power to manufacture and remanufacture ourselves through better images? Have we not in fact become like the gods? Do we not possess great powers along very limited technological dimensions and hence like the gods lack the accompanying moral and political dimensions to put our new powers in proper perspective?

Concluding Remarks

The rules by which TV operates cannot be seen directly. The rules behind all of the seductive images, the glitter— in short, the gloss that tempts us into throwing aside older versions of reality in the relentless pursuit of new or better improved ones—cannot be seen. The paradox is that for a medium that is primarily visual, TV can show everything except the rules by which it operates. And this is surely not because everything we've talked about in this chapter couldn't be shown—indeed, all the mechanisms of unreality we've discussed would make a fascinating TV program in itself—but because TV has a vested interest in not showing them. Which is a far different matter from saying that people wouldn't watch such a program if it were produced.

The last two chapters have argued that there is a coherence to unreality. It is not a random, chaotic, unorganized phenomenon. How could it be when, like all other phenomena, it is created by people? As we discovered long ago, anything done by people almost by definition must contain some order. It's either the order of intentional consciousness or that of unintentional unconsciousness.

We here must say a few words about the distinction between pseudo reality or what in Chapter One we called Unreality Two and artificial reality or what we referred to as Unreality One. We earlier defined Unreality Two as the deliberate distortion of complexity and in this sense reality. *Artificial reality, or Unreality One, really sits halfway between reality and unreality.* Indeed, artificial reality can be thought of as the handservant of either reality or unreality.[16]

Artificial reality is the simulation, mainly via computers, of the most complex features of man's "natural" environment. The purpose of such simulations is to allow men and women to practice in carefully controlled situations what would be far too dangerous for them to do in uncontrolled situations, for example, piloting commercial aircraft without long hours of training.[17] As the power of computers and sophistication of graphic displays have both increased enormously, artificial realities have become more lifelike in the features they contain. Hence, not only do they allow people to experiment with ordinary reality but they have even begun to surpass ordinary reality itself by creating new (artificial) realities. Thus, our contention is that artificial reality sits midway between reality and unreality for it can be used both to explore and to develop either one. If our society appears increasingly headed in the direction of unreality, then artificial reality is the midwife bringing it to life.

A final comment: In the 19th century, the fundamental philosophical debate—dialectic—was between free will and determinism. As a creature in God's likeness, did man possess a soul and a will that were autonomous, or, as a member of the physical universe was man's behavior completely describable in physical terms? In other words, was man really free to plan his actions or was freedom an illusion? The dialectic between free will and determinism in its original form is no longer as relevant for us in this century although it can never be fully dismissed or dealt with completely.

The fundamental dialectic for our time is between reality and unreality, especially now that we have the power to influence and create both. Will both grow equally or will one exert a decisive influence over the other? What, in short, is to be the fate of man? What side of the dialectic will win out, the ability of man to face directly and honestly the complex realities he's capable of creating, or, the ability of man to turn away from reality and to invest his energy increasingly in the denial of reality?

> What happens if CBS has one of these machines that can generate real-time animation of photographic quality? You look at two TVs—one has got a picture of Ronald Reagan shaking hands with Gorbachev, and the other set has a picture of Ronald Reagan punching Gorbachev in the nose, and you can't tell them apart. One is on videotape and one was synthesized on a computer. We already don't believe in film anymore. *What's going to happen to electronic news gathering when the validating function of videotape no longer exists* [emphasis ours]? Television will no longer be a verification medium. Who's going to control that?
>
> How do we put governors [i.e., in our language, "guarantors"] on these fantasy systems so that people don't fantasize the wrong things?[18]

5. The Industrialized Perfection of Rottenness

...the businessperson who uses celebrity, the entertainer who seeks it, and the individual who is confronted by it—show just how far celebrity has spread into every sector of American life. So great is the value of visibility that the manufacturing and marketing of celebrities now reaches into business, sports, entertainment, religion, the arts, politics, academics, medicine, and the law. Visibility is what every aspiring hostess wants, what every professional seeks. It is the crucial ingredient that can make lawyer X the most sought after in town, talk show host Y the most popular in her market, and surgeon Z the most highly paid in his city. *This is the potential of industrialized celebrity manufacturing, the potential for elevating virtually anyone to a level of visibility unimaginable in any other age—and compensating that individual with unimaginable rewards* [italics ours]....

Today, there is a whole industry that manages the business of transforming unknowns into celebrities, changing virtually every element of personality, appearance, and character that it is possible to change.

> ...*They are manufactured, just as are cars, clothes, and computers* [italics in original].

> —Irving J. Rein, et al., *High Visibility*, pp.3-6

A Manual for Celebrityhood

George Santayana once remarked that certain books were best regarded as outstanding examples of the perfection of rottenness. They should be read, if at all, with an attitude of fascination, much as one views the scene of a heinous crime with feelings that alternate between horror, curiosity, and disgust. Were he alive today, Santayana would surely regard the book *High Visibility*[1] as a supreme example of what he had in mind.

A veritable manual for the manufacturing of celebrities, *High Visibility* offers an application of all the latest techniques of "marketing science" to celebrityhood. We predict it will become a classic of its kind. Its subtitle alone is revealing; *How Executives, Politicians, Entertainers, Athletes, and Other Professionals Create, Market, and Achieve Successful Images*.

If the subtitle of *High Visibility* indicates clearly why it stands at one end of the spectrum, then that of Richard Schickel's *Intimate Strangers*[2] illustrates why it stands at the other: *The Culture of Celebrity, How Our National Obsession With Celebrity Shapes Our World and Bends Our Mind*. Precisely because they differ so much, both books together offer an illuminating exercise in surfacing the mechanisms that underlie the celebrity production industry. Taken together, they constitute a natural dialectic and reveal more clearly the mechanisms that are at the heart of the celebrity industry than if merely one alone were available.

Where *Intimate Strangers* regards those mechanisms with horror and contempt, *High Visibility* not only adopts a matter-of-fact attitude towards them but exhibits an admiration that most narrow professionals adopt towards the tools of their trade. They are enamored of the technical excellence of their tools without an enlightened concern for their broader social implications. In fact, the harshest criticisms of *High Visibility* are directed towards media critics such as Schickel who presumably fail to appreciate what the celebrity industry is trying to accomplish, who fail to achieve a true appreciation of the mechanisms for their own sake; they should stop their complaining because of their presumed jealousy at their having failed to achieve the same degree of fame as those of whom they are critical:

> ...While our social critics attack the highly visible and denounce them as undeserving of their tremendous salaries, power, privilege, and control over society's opinions, what the critics *really* seem to be angry about is that they themselves don't control the process. Critics of celebrity culture will never be able to control image formation. The root causes of why people want—indeed, *need*—celebrities are so basic as to render the critics' complaints superfluous. That the public chooses to worship David Bowie and not the editor of *Commentary* is not necessarily destructive or damaging. It is, to the contrary, often valuable and certainly worth understanding.[3]

A book that embodies the perfection of rottenness and an industry whose core is founded on that rottenness are two very different things. For this reason alone, were Santayana alive today he would probably be even more concerned about the current state of rottenness for its ante has clearly been raised.

The purpose of this chapter is to show that the production and consumption of unreality has clearly reached the industrialized stage, and further, that its end results are far from being trivial. Indeed, two major consequences result from the industrialization of unreality. One, the techniques and strategies for celebrity development have shifted dramatically as the industry itself has "matured" over the course of this century; in brief, there has been a clear shift from the discovery and development of people who had raw talent to begin with to the stage where the possession of raw talent is almost irrelevant to celebrity-hood. Two, the industrialized production of celebrities reveals that there is a definite, dark, Orwellian side to unreality. Contrary to Neil Postman,[4] the production and consumption of almost unlimited amounts of mindless entertainment is not harmless, amusing, or banal.

What Makes Anything an Industry?

When we think of an industry, the manufacture of steel, cars, or electronics usually comes to mind. An industry is much broader than a single company. Typically, a number of different companies are involved, most of which are in competition with one another. If the industry is big enough, it usually has a trade association to represent its interests against the government and other industries.

There is no clear-cut, dividing line between what is or isn't an industry. However, an industry usually possesses a much more elaborate infrastructure than an individual company does. An industry typically involves a much more complex, elaborate, sophisticated, specialized set of activities.

To see what an industry is, let's first examine a powerful way of characterizing what a company is. The concept of *stakeholders*[5] is one of the most important ways of visualizing a company. Essentially, a stakeholder is *any* single individual, group, organization, or social entity that either *affects* or is in turn *affected by* the policies of an organization, industry, or social entity. Whether they are literally inside or outside an organization, stakeholders have a *direcct stake* in its behavior, actions, and policies. Figure 1 gives a simple example.

To understand the meaning and implications, consider the following, typical situation. Suppose a drug company wants to bring out a new drug at a certain price. Two interrelated decisions are involved: whether to launch the new drug in the first place, and what price to charge for the drug for maximum profits to the company. Both decisions or company policies involve considerations among the various players or stakeholders in Figure 1.

Each of the various stakeholders can have a major impact on the decision of the company represented by the central circle. For instance, if one brings out the new drug

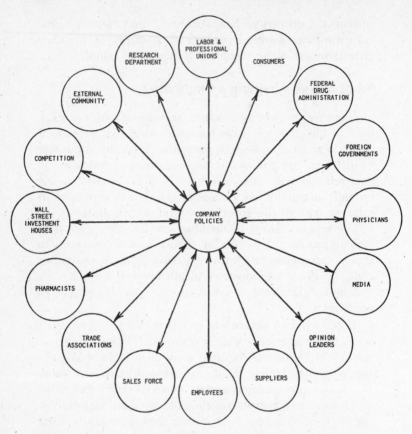

Figure 1. A Typical Stakeholder Map for a Pharmaceutical Company.

at a certain price, will the competition respond? Will they introduce a competing drug at a cheaper price? Can the new drug get easy Federal Drug Administration approval? Will consumers easily adopt it or do they have considerable loyalty to another brand? Will physicians appreciate the drug's new benefits enough so that they will recommend it to their patients? Will the media respond favorably to the new brand? Do the company and its people have a history of good relations with the media so that they can draw upon it? Or was the company involved in shady dealings in the past so that it has a tarnished image?

All these questions and more are highly critical. They are enough to show that anything any company or institution does in the modern world influences and is influenced by a multitude of stakeholders both internal and external. In fact, harkening back to Chapter Two, one of the reasons why the world is so much more complex than it was even 20 years ago is that there are so many more *organized* stakeholder groups that impact any organization. For example: gay and lesbian groups impact the general hiring, health, and AIDS policies and attitudes of organizations; environmental defense and activist groups impact not only the decision where to locate plants, but also the company's manufacturing policies, and so forth.

Even worse, the number, variety, and complexity of different stakeholder groups is such that no one can know for sure who they are (i.e., who will surface around a particular issue) and how they will behave prior to the introduction of the drug. Of necessity then, every organization has to make a bunch of highly critical, uncertain *assumptions* prior to the appearance of the drug. In effect, how will the various stakeholders behave? They differ in the amounts of their holdings, the kind of power they possess, their ability to affect other stakeholders, their access to information, money and resources in general, etc. As a result, the assumptions made with regard to stakeholders are so critical that they affect every aspect of the drug's manufacturing, distribution, and pricing. Yet, they cannot be identified for certain either prior to the drug's debut, or strangely enough, often even after its appearance on the market. Many a company has been burned seriously because it neglected to consider a particular stakeholder as relevant to its situation or it seriously underestimated the stakeholder's impact. For example, what effect Consumer's Union, the publisher of the highly influential *Consumer Reports*, would have on the sale of Suzuki Samurai jeeps in the United States as a result of its report on the vehicles' reputed poor safety record.

In addition, businesses in recent years have witnessed the emergence of a whole new class of stakeholders with whom they have never before had to deal, or at least not on the same scale. The natures of these additional stakeholders are indicated in Figure 2. They represent the dark or the unconscious side of every organization and its policies;[6] "unconscious" because they have mainly been unnecessary to consider as major forces in previous years; "dark" because they represent the potentially evil side of every organization. Consider as one example the terrifying phenomenon of product tampering.

There is a deep paradox associated with every business, but especially with those whose products are taken for health or nutritional reasons. If a health or nutritional

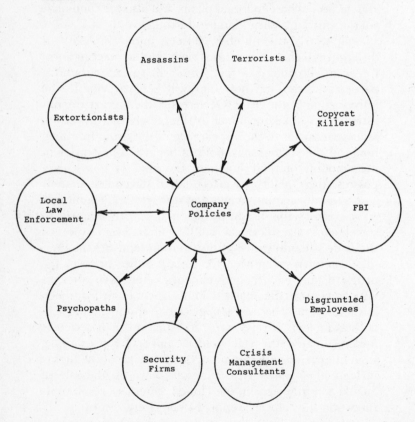

Figure 2.

product becomes highly successful, then it is potentially capable of becoming a lethal weapon for accomplishing widespread social harm.[7] If the product is tampered with through, say, the introduction of cyanide by an extortionist, psychopath, etc., then a number of critical policy questions face an organization: (1) should we withdraw our product from the marketplace; (2) if we decide to withdraw, how extensively should it be withdrawn; (3) is a nationwide recall warranted or merely a more confined local one; (4) will the company be blamed for negligence if we didn't recall when we should have, i.e., if someone is harmed or killed; (5) on the other hand, if we do withdraw when we don't need to, will we needlessly lose millions of dollars; and (6) if we do withdraw, will we encourage other terrorists, psychopaths, copycat killers, and extortionists to make similar threats in the future? Because there are no easy answers to these questions, they are more critical than ever. (It is beyond the scope of this book to demonstrate how such questions can be treated, but they can. New methods have been developed in recent years which allow one to deal with these and other messy problems in a systematic fashion.[8])

With these concepts as background, we are able to do three things. We can show the evolution of the unreality industry over time. We can show the development of its corresponding policies for creating celebrities. And we can show in a much more systematic fashion than has been done before, the Dark Side of the unreality industry.

The Evolution of the Celebrity Manufacturing Industry

When we speak of unreality as an industry, it is enough to demonstrate what this means in terms of the manufacturing of celebrities. As we remarked, the structure of the celebrity manufacturing industry has changed drastically over the course of this century. In general, the development of the industry parallels that of most other industries. Its complexity has increased steadily over time, and is in direct proportion to the number of specialized stakeholders involved in the manufacturing process and the greater number of advanced technologies that can be employed.

Figures 3 through 6 show the evolution of the industry.[9] Generally speaking, the differences between Figures 3 through 6 involve the degree to which an aspirant is transformed in the process of becoming a celebrity.

Figure 3 describes the earliest model of the industry. Here, the aspirant is essentially taken as "given." Friends or families respond initially to the immediate performances of a potential "star" and encourage him or her to develop their talents further. In this model, the would-be celebrity is not transformed so much as his or her talents are perfected through training. It is mainly up to the

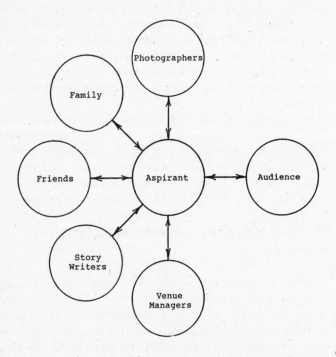

Figure 3. The Cottage Stage of Celebrity Manufacturing.

aspirant to seek out teachers, arrange for photographs and write-ups and to distribute them to venue managers— those who control theaters or other places where the talents of a potential aspirant are likely to be showcased. In other words, in the cottage industry stage, potential celebrity aspirants are developed and/or promoted largely by a personal cadre of teachers, friends, or parents.

These "helpers" in turn seek out dancing teachers, dramatic coaches, lawyers, etc. Thus, the celebrity aspirant's personal helpers seek and arrange by themselves the appropriate lessons for the aspirant. Under this plan of proceeding, the aspirant depends largely on developing whatever talents he or she has and hopes, through hard work and luck, to be "discovered." A number of plucky individuals still continue to make use of this model although fewer use it each year since its success rate is too low to justify the expenditures of time, energy, and money it requires.

Figure 4 represents the next stage in the development of the industry. Under this model, we begin to see the utilization of more specialists to help refine the aspirant's talents and to bring him or her to the attention of the outside world. This represents the industrializing stage. The most common specialists hired here are agents, publicists, and lawyers who in turn will refer the aspirant to further professional help from coaches, teachers, accountants, and so on. The specialists may even work with the communications media to spread the potential celebrity's image to the outside world and hence further the promotion and development of the aspirant.

Figure 5 represents the real breakthrough to an out-and-out organized industry. This stage is not only a much more advanced and sophisticated version of the previous one (see Figure 4), but in this model, every brand of expertise necessary to spot, develop, market, and sell new celebrities *is brought under one centralized roof.* For instance, specialists who can "teach charisma" by breaking it down into carefully designed stages are employed. New names and story lines for potential aspirants will be designed in-house. Clinical psychologists might be employed to transform the

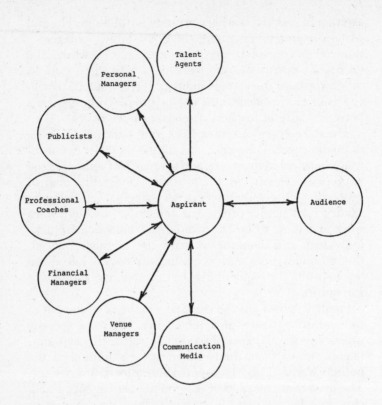

Figure 4. The Industrializing Stage of Celebrity Manufacturing.

individual's personality to be completely consistent and consonant with the story line. An entire strategy for the transformation of the aspirant and his or her careful development in controlled settings will be painstakingly developed. If need be, every facet of the aspirant's life from his or her finances to where they live, how they dress, what they eat, with whom they are seen, etc., will be carefully developed and coordinated.

With this model, the process of celebrity manufacturing thus takes a definite turn. It represents a real point of no return to the earlier models. Market researchers are employed to find out what the public wants from celebrities.

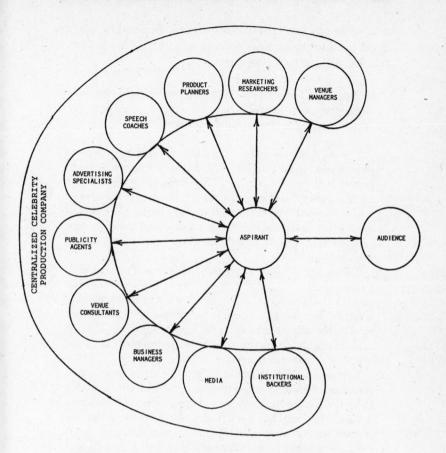

Figure 5. The Factory Stage of Celebrity Manufacturing.

These in turn are translated into specs to see if there is a potential celebrity in-house who already meets the criteria or whether a potential aspirant is malleable enough to be manufactured to fit the specifications as to what the public wants. In this stage, marketing becomes a dominant factor or consideration. Different marketing segments and sectors are identified in their order of performance, i.e., drawing power. Story lines are also carefully crafted to establish an identity for the potential aspirant. Celebrities are not only given new names to fit their new identities, but new identities are fashioned for them. Depending on how deep the internalization process is, in effect a whole new "packaged" identity is created:

Suppose a female pop singer, unable to obtain booking engagements on her own, hires an agent to help her. The agent faces three basic strategy options:

1. *Pure selling approach.* Here the agent would present photos and tapes of the singer to several venue managers to persuade them to book her. The singer is satisfied if her agent succeeds, and she is extremely satisfied if the venues are prestigious, visible, or well paying. In the pure selling mode, the agent sees the client as a fixed product that simply has to be sold, as is, to the "best" market that can be found.

2. *Product improvement approach.* Not content to work with a fixed quantity, here the agent takes an inventory of the singer's characteristics and suggests ways in which she can improve her songs, appearance, personality, and other modifiable characteristics. The agent is taking a value added approach—adding value to the performer's ability to attract the market's interest.

3. *Market fulfillment approach.* Here the agent decides that the singer does not possess the minimum skills or flexibility to be sold as is or molded into a viable product. So the agent declines to help her specifically. Instead, he scans the market seeing what kind of public entertainment needs exist and are not being adequately satisfied. The scan may reveal that the market is ready for, perhaps, another Anne Murray-type singer. The agent then searches among the pool of minimally qualified aspirants for the one who is most promotable into this role. Finding the right person, the agent proceeds to develop her systematically into a new Anne Murray—the product the market wants.

Today, the same three marketing styles are in use in the non-entertainment sectors. In the political sector, the pure selling approach means trying to attract more votes for existing candidates as they are; the key is to create in the voters an attraction to the qualities and characteristics that the candidate already possesses. In the product improvement approach, the candidate is transformed—trained to speak more effectively, dress more in line with the audiences' (voters') expectations, and expressed views shown by polling to already be popular. The third approach, market fulfillment, is used, if discreetly, by political machines and parties to analyze what the public wants in the way of public officials and find candidates who meet voter desires and expectations.

Already, today's political parties are becoming more sophisticated, moving steadily toward the market fulfillment approach, searching for potential candidates who can fulfill market expectations.... With the stakes riding so high in the launch of a major aspirant, new style celebrity makers are increasingly turning to such modern marketing tools as audience analysis, public opinion research, and focus groups, in which a selected group of consumers is deeply probed to reveal their views on products, services, and celebrities.[10]

Through the use of modern marketing techniques, it has been established that very few stars have the ability to appeal to all market sectors or segments of the population. Indeed, it has been possible to identify in their order of importance—their potential for widespread audience identification and appeal—the following key sectors from which celebrities can come and in turn make their pitch to:

1. Entertainment
2. Sports
3. Politics
4. The General Culture
5. Business
6. Religion
7. Science
8. The Professions
9. Academia.[11]

In addition to identifying the above nine key sectors, 22 major story lines have also been identified that have been used successfully in the past to fashion the general identity of a celebrity. The stories are so prominent that it's easy to list the name of some famous celebrity who has used the story line successfully to catapult himself or herself to fame. The titles of the stories literally speak for themselves:

1. *First of a Kind*: Geraldine Ferraro
2. *Talent Wins Out*: Barbra Streisand
3. *Success/Adversity/Success*: Tina Turner
4. *The Fatal Flaw*: Ted Kennedy and Chappaquidick
5. *Restrained From Greatness*: Loretta Lynn
6. *A Great Rivalry*: Tennis Players Bjorn Borg and John McEnroe
7. *Mom's or Dad's Footsteps*: Julian Lennon
8. *The Big Break*: Whoopi Goldberg and *The Color Purple*
9. *The Accidental Meeting*: Diana Ross and The Jackson Five
10. *The Great Teacher*: Norman Vincent Peale and Robert Schuler
11. *Moved by Religious Power*: Oral Roberts
12. *The Great Sacrifice*: Vincent Van Gogh
13. *The Incredible Feat*: Peter Uberroth Masterminding the Olympics
14. *Young Dramatic Death*: James Dean
15. *Small Person Takes Over Big Office*: Coach Jerry Faust at Notre Dame
16. *The Pure Archetype*: Lieutenant Colonel Oliver North
17. *Revenge*: Lee Iacocca (against Henry Ford for firing him)
18. *Need to Prove Something*: Maria Schriver
19. *Risks All*: Ivan Boesky
20. *Pawn in a Game*: Former *Playboy* Bunny Dorothy Stratten Murdered by Her Ex-Lover
21. *Outrageous Behavior*: *Hustler* Magazine Publisher Larry Flynt
22. *Little Guy Makes Good*: Woody Allen.[12]

It is important to understand the reasons for the development of the industry over time. With its specialized functions the industry's increased development is a partial reflection of the inefficiency of the earliest model in fulfilling the widespread demand that has been created for celebrities. The first model not only is inefficient in sorting out the truly talented from the mediocre, but is essentially reactive. It doesn't take the next step of developing people proactively who may or may not be genuinely talented but, more important, can be molded enough to meet audience expectations. To appreciate the full ramifications of this, it is necessary to have some understanding as to why celebrityhood has become so powerful a force in our time.

Celebrityhood by and large did not exist prior to this century. For most of human history, the vast numbers of people had little, if virtually no, direct contact with those who occupied high places. Most people would not even be so fortunate as to secure a once-in-a-lifetime, fleeting glimpse of someone famous. It was only in this century with the invention of widespread, rapid means of travel, communication, and photography that ordinary people could begin to see those that they had only dreamt of previously.

The "big breakthrough" occurred arguably with the invention of motion pictures. People could now see portrayed on a regular basis those they only could fantasize about in the past. Every aspect of their being was magnified a hundred times on a huge screen. The invention of the close-up shot made much of this possible.[13]

Nowadays, we take such inventions so much for granted that we forget that, like most things, the close-up shot is not a natural way to view our fellow man. It is an artifact, an invention, that was made possible by the medium of motion pictures. Thus, the camera focused in on the eyes, the lips, the hair, the bosoms of our heroes and heroines in ways that we never saw one another before. Seeing such things on a week-in week-out basis one cannot help developing an intense curiosity about what these people are like in other settings, how they live, what and whom they like, what they wear, eat, dream. One cannot, in short, form an intense bond with such people without indulging in deep fantasies about them. It is precisely the human ability to fantasize that lies at the heart of nearly all the forces that Freud identified which move the human psyche.

Since the real life stories of the stars were not always as interesting—or as plentiful—as those demanded by the ever curious public, many had to be manufactured. Their truth was not necessary, only their believability in the sense that they fitted in with and contributed to the persona, the star image. In the beginning, Hollywood was a novice at story production but it quickly learned to apply its on-screen story writing talents to the off-screen lives of its stars. A new genre was mastered—pseudo stories, which in turn gave rise to pseudo events, i.e., staged events that had as their only purpose the creation of artificial newsworthy happenings so that the star could be widely observed by his/her adoring publics.

Fame and accomplishment, which had not always gone hand in hand, even in previous centuries, began to diverge. *One of the consequences of the constant need for inventing stories that bore little relation to the actual personalities or lives of stars was to effect a growing separation between fame or celebrityhood and actual accomplishment. Fame not only came to bear less and less relationship to actual accomplishment but actual accomplishment itself beccame an impediment to fame.* The gifted or accomplished became a threat to the average person, for whom, as a result, the stars were deliberately created so that the masses could live out their fantasies. The process of intense identification was made infinitely easier if the stars were different but "not too different" from their adoring fans, who could fantasize that each star was a more glamorous version of themselves. Besides, fame itself is hard enough to handle on its own. If, however, the famous were also genuinely competent, then this contributed even further to their danger through the intense passions unleashed by feelings of envy. More than once, envy has been motive enough to stir the less famous to assassination or murder.

The last stage in the development of the celebrity industry (Figure 6) indicates where it is clearly heading; having reached the point where it only exists as part of an entire network of highly related industries. The process of manufacturing and promoting celebrities is now so big and so complicated that it requires the intense cooperation of

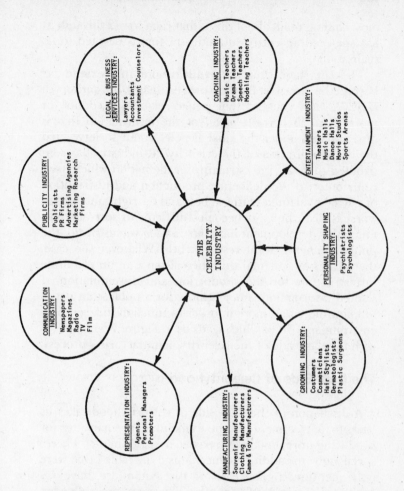

Figure 6. The Structure of the Celebrity Manufacturing Industry.

other industries in order for it to operate. It is thus impossible to say any longer where the industry clearly begins and where it leaves off. This is the stage of the deepest interpenetration of the industry with society. It is also the stage where the more severe forms of personality alteration are involved. These were merely mentioned in Table 1 of Chapter Four (rows 2 through 5). (For ease of discussion, this table is reproduced on the next page.) The most chilling point about this is that each row (2 through 5) has spawned an entire sub-industry that is devoted to its realization.

The last stage thus has ramifications that extend far beyond the industry. By their own estimates, the authors of *High Visibility* contend that public relations accounts for more than 70 percent of all of the information that is disseminated under the label as news in our society. That the decentralization of the celebrity/PR industry has contributed to a vast infrastructure in the nation which itself contributes to the deliberate production and distribution of partial or slanted truths at best and outright untruths at worst is disturbing. It becomes difficult to sort out how much this development has *contributed to* versus *created* the public's general disinterest in truth. Whatever the case, there can be no denial that the existence of an elaborate infrastructure for the production and dissemination of slanted information is not healthy for a public that needs to know more and more in order to function in a complex environment. All of which leads us to Figure 7 which deals with the dark side of the celebrity manufacturing process.

The Dark Side of Celebrityhood

A discussion of the dark side of celebrityhood takes us back to a treatment of the remaining mechanisms for producing unreality that we passed over in Chapter Three: specifically, the additional mechanisms in Table 1 that were only mentioned. For ease of discussion, we have reproduced Table 1 of Chapter Three on the following pages. To appreciate the nature of these additional mechanisms, it is necessary to discuss something of the history of fame.

To say that celebrityhood is a relatively recent invention is far different from saying the same thing of fame, which, clearly, is as old as human history. Even as sensitive and acute a student of fame as Richard Schickel misses a fundamental point that many of the properties he ascribes to fame in general, and celebrityhood in particular, as being distinctive of the 20th century have in actuality

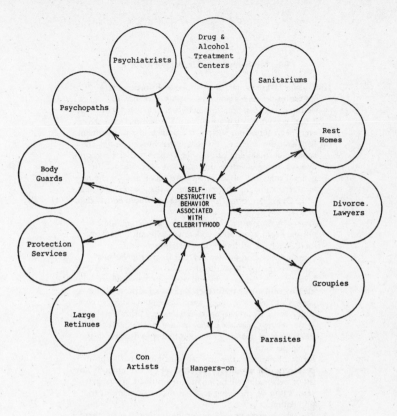

Figure 7. A Map of the Dark Side of Celebrityhood.

existed in previous centuries as well. Like all things human, fame has a complex history.[14] Further, its dimensions vary enormously from culture to culture and from time period to time period. Some of fame's properties have remained constant throughout the centuries; thus, our period differs only in degree but not fundamentally in kind with regard to some of these characteristics. Other properties, however, are radically different today. To differentiate between those that remain the same versus those that have changed requires knowledge of fame's history.

It is not, however, the purpose of this book to present this history in depth. For our purposes, it merely suffices to

TABLE 1

The Mechanisms for Unreality Production

(1) *Boundary Warping*, i.e., the deliberate distortion and
    confusion between traditional realms of reality, for
    example, between entertainment and news; the general rule
    is that everything that appears on TV, and increasingly in
    every segment of our society, is a branch of entertainment;

(2) *Image Engineering*, i.e., any image that human beings are
    capable of imagining can now be constructed electronically
    and is capable of interacting with any other image; the
    general rules are: (a) all images are equal, and (b) the more
    bizarre the image, "the more equal," the "better" the image
    is; in Orwellian terms, some images are "more equal" than
    others;

(3) *Personality Fragmentation or Splitting of the Person*, ideas are
    not only split apart and rendered incoherent on TV and
    increasingly on all forms of entertainment and
    communication in our society, but so are the various
    aspects of people; thus, isolated individual body parts (e.g.,
    breasts, faces, noses, hair, and teeth, etc.) assume an
    identity of their own; further, individual aspects of the
    person's psyche (e.g., ego), specific emotions (e.g., greed,
    anger, love), or archetypal characters (e.g., the Warrior as
    in the movie *Conan the Barbarian*) are also isolated and
    treated out of any larger context that would relate to the
    whole person;

(4) *Person Engineering*, the general principle is that a specific
    person can be manufactured or made over to embody any
    set of personality characteristics determined by market
    research to be appealing to a significant segment of the
    population;

(5) *The Disconnectedness of Ideas*, on the surface at least, there is
    little, if any, connection between the ideas that float off
    TV or the other segments of our society; no connecting
    thread, overall context, or historical perspective is provided
    that would help the viewer, reader, audience, etc., make
    any sense of the larger pattern of ideas, images, etc.,
    assuming that there was one, that would tie all of the
    images or ideas together into any coherent whole;

(6) *A Self-Sealing Universe*, the general principle is that TV and
    increasingly all the other forms of communication in our
    society, refer less and less to anything outside of their own
    artificially, self-constructed, self-contained world; the result
    is that virtually all of the forms of unreality have become
    almost totally capable of incorporating any criticism
    directed against them by including those very criticisms

into their day to day operations; thus, TV shows and commercials of all kinds, for instance the popular Joe Isuzu ads, incorporate the very cynicism against the media into its operations;

(7) *Personality Reduction*, everything is personality on TV and in the general entertainment society of America; abstract ideas tend not to exist; they exist only if they can be represented in a concrete person; for example, Einstein is the personal embodiment of the intellectual, Joan Collins is the archetypal bitch, etc.;

(8) *Radical Simplification*, all forms of unreality have no room for abstract ideas; they have even less for complex ones; for instance, everything on TV and in popular books must be simplified up to and beyond the point of trivialization; the result is TV and contemporary American culture not only constitute a vast wasteland on the landscape of history, but worse yet, they constitute one of the largest efforts in programmatic ignorance or unreality creation on the face of the planet;

(9) *Instant Means for Celebrityhood,* one of the most disturbing aspects of unreality is that the psychopath may understand better than those who supposedly have a grip on so-called "normal" reality the means for achieving instantaneous celebrityhood, i.e., the murder and assassination of someone else who is already a celebrity;

(10) *Reverse Causality*, TV has rendered traditional causality, i.e., the traditional sequence of events, irrelevent; TV sound plays a highly important role in this process; for this very reason, its role is often overlooked; TV sound summons the passive viewer/listener back to the set to watch a rewinding of an "important event"; e.g., first a touchdown (or an important political event, news story) is scored, then we watch in reverse sequence what "caused it," only the "cause" in this case now becomes the "effect";

(11) *The Decentralized Industrial Stage of Unreality Production*, celebrities are the chief products of an entire industry and the industry has advanced to the next stage in its development; celebrities can now be literally manufactured from nearly any part of the country; it is no longer necessary to move to New York, L.A., or Nashville to name a few of the previously centralized locations from where celebrities could once only be produced;

(12) *Infrastructure Penetration and Contamination*, the manufacturing of unreality has reached such proportions that it has literally infiltrated itself into virtually every aspect of U.S. life; the phenomenon is thus so deeply and widely entrenched into the very lifeblood of U.S. society that its eradication is highly problematic at this point.

note some of its highlights. For instance, fame begins to receive its first clear definition in Greece some five hundred years before the birth of Christ. Alexander the Great, certainly one of the pivotal figures in the history of fame, not only reveals the early Greek character of fame—to be famous in Greek society is to be a figure totally unprecedented—but he displays one of the central characteristics that nearly all aspirants to fame have displayed down through the centuries. Alexander constantly manipulates the story of his background in order to make his image loom larger in life even though his actual accomplishments were sufficient to speak for themselves.

The early history of fame also reveals the vast differences in its definition and manifestation in different cultures. Whereas fame in early Greece meant one was a character without precedent, fame in early Rome meant that one was one of the best, if not most perfect, public expressions of the values of his class.[15] Thus, Roman fame is essentially political whereas Greek fame is essentially aesthetic and spiritual. Although it is true that contemporary society has, far more than earlier societies, widened the gap between legitimate fame—that which is based on actual accomplishment—and manipulated fame, in the fame-oriented society of early Rome it was no less difficult to distinguish between the two. The preoccupation with fame in Roman society was in fact overriding to the most prominent citizens. To be prominent in Rome was to actively court public display. For instance, it is not true that only in our times are the famous preoccupied with how their deaths can be turned into a media event or that they themselves will be turned into one by the media (e.g., Marilyn Monroe, Liberace, Rock Hudson, Natalie Wood):

> ...In the moment of his assassination, stabbed twenty-three times, yet, as Suetonius describes, with the self consciousness that never left him, Caesar fell, arranging his toga so that even in death he would have control over his image. With remarkable speed, he had defined a way of being in public that his enemies could do little to change.[16]

Suetonius's account of his death indicates how deeply in him this urge ran:

On the day that he died, Augustus frequently inquired whether rumors of his illness were causing any popular disturbance. He called for a mirror, and had his hair combed and his lower jaw, which had fallen from weakness, propped up. Presently, he summoned a group of friends and asked: "Have I played my part in the farce of life credibly enough?" adding the threatrical tag:

> If I have pleased you, kindly signify
> Appreciation with a warm good-
> bye...

Finally, he kissed his wife with: "Good-bye, Livia: Never forget whose spouse you have been," and died almost at once.

No Shakespearian actor king could have left the stage better.[17]

What is certainly true of modern times is that fame, especially in America, is the product of three major forces: American history (as well as its antecedents in general European and especially in British history), American culture, and modern technology. It is not possible to understand the role that celebrities, especially their deliberate manufacturing, play in contemporary America without understanding something of the historical forces that have peculiarly shaped America. For instance, the writings of John Locke played a critical role in shaping American government. From Locke, we inherited the notion that one of the chief functions of government was the protection of property. From this, it was but a short series of steps to the translation of this notion into "a citizen was a man *of property*." Given this, it is only a further series of short steps to "a man *is* his property"; and finally to "a man *is property*, i.e., an object himself." But if so, why not improve then on the fundamental property itself, i.e., persons, through the intervention of technology? Why not allow each individual to redesign himself/herself to the specs of the day so that each might then really engage in the pursuit of happiness with a vengeance?

In America especially, if all men were created equal, then fame was potentially equally, democratically open to all. We have, in short, with the appearance of America the democratization of fame. Further, if all men were endowed with the inalienable right to the pursuit of happiness, then in effect didn't the Founding Fathers give each person a mandate to pursue his/her self-fulfillment? And increasingly doesn't self-fulfillment mean the right to self development? And doesn't self development go hand in hand with the American tradition of self-made men so that if one didn't like the form that one's creator had dished out, wasn't one entitled to make oneself over entirely? In short, isn't the tradition of self-made an injunction—a moral license—to use the latest technology to completely remake oneself?

An important consequence follows almost immediately. The ever greater and continually growing distance or lack of connection between fame and actual accomplishment contributed to the phenomenon of Boundary Warping that we talked about in Chapter Three. The growing *separation* between fame and accomplishment actually made possible the *blurring* of the boundaries between "reality" and fiction that was to become pronounced in the latter part of the 20th century.

Other consequences followed as well. These result in the other mechanisms that were skimmed over in Chapter Three (see Table 1 of Chapter Three reprinted in this chapter). A deep sense of mystery has always been an important ingredient of real art. A true piece of art is never fully explainable. This is one of the reasons why we are continually drawn to it again and again. But such mystery will not do for the masses who, as we noted in Chapter Two, regard any sign or source of complexity or ambivalence as a sign of weakness. Thus, mystery, like truth itself had to be cheapened, i.e., trivialized, if celebrityhood and unreality were to flourish. Thus in our time mystery has been reduced to such banalities as "does she or doesn't she; only her hairdresser knows."

Truth and artistic criticism, which also go hand in hand, had to be killed as well. For the function of the critic is assessment and pointing out where inferior art is lacking both in truth and in mystery. Thus, "artists" like Andy Warhol had to be created and/or created themselves on the basis of dispelling mystery. Their works were supremely accessible to an audience that had no tolerance for "deeper mystery and higher truths."

The end result is the appearance of books such as *High Visibility*. They are merely the latest inheritors of a long tradition which has always stressed that truth or criticism are irrelevant, if not dangerous, to the manufacturing of celebrities. True to their own dictum of the irrelevancy of truth, such books never tell the full story about fame. Either out of ignorance or deliberate falsification, they tell only one side at best. They suppress the full history and nature of fame. If they did not, then they would be forced to present both sides of the picture *side by side* as Table 2 attempts to do—to paint a more balanced portrait of the presumed benefits versus the potential costs of fame. It is the general tendency of ideologues, especially technological ones, to see only the presumed positive benefits. Almost by definition, technologists are almost incapable of seeing the negative side and hence the full picture.

Hundreds of personal stories could be used to illustrate the "dark side" of celebrityhood. The dark side is itself so prevalent and so much an ever present companion to celebrityhood that it is often used to promote the last hurrah of a waining celebrity's career. More often than not, it represents the final act of a genuine tragedy. For example, former NBC anchorwoman Jessica Savitch is the subject of several recently published "postmortems."

As *Los Angeles Times* TV critic Howard Rosenberg has put it, "Savitch's story is one more example of how TV executives too often sell news by selling the personalities who deliver news:

> Savitch was only 30 when hired by NBC News as a weekend anchor in 1977 after a sizzling local news career at KHOU in Houston and KAYW in Philadelphia. No matter that she wasn't qualified for network-level journalism. NBC and its affiliate stations saw in Savitch all the qualifications they needed to see. They saw rating points.
>
> The later, torturous stages of Savitch's career were a tribute to fiscal and human waste. Paradoxically, she was making a handsome $315,000 a year when she died, but she

TABLE 2

THE LEDGER SHEET OF FAME

The Presumed Benefits of Fame		The Potential Costs of Fame	
Confers *Power*, Self-Control, Self-Determination Power of > Power of Famous Public	As the world has become more complex, the power of the single individual has decreased steadily; fame promises liberation from powerless anonymity, from the painful death of being unknown.	Confers *Entrapment*, Beholden to Others Power of > Power of Public Famous	Increased visibility, self-exposure, not only increases one's physical vulnerability but one's psychological dependence on an audience whose whims are often arbitrary and capricious.
Attainment of Perfection, *Fills Up the Holes* in One's Self, Satisfies the Hunger Within	Fame gives one entree into a world where supposedly all of one's blemishes are removed, all psychic wounds are healed; all self doubts are removed.	Often Creates *Bigger Holes* Leading to Self-Destruction, the Hunger Only Gets Bigger	Fame often increases one's self doubts; one can never really be sure that one is liked, loved, respected for one's true, inner self; fame often leads to suicide as the only remaining act of true heroism or authenticity left; fame is often a never ending hunger (famine) that can never be satisfied; more fame only increases the need for even more.

Ultimate *Acceptance* into a Special Community Fame leads to acceptance into a special, mystical-like community of other famous people.	Ultimate *Rejection*, Continual Jockeying for Position, Constant Need to Prove One Is Worthy to the Community	Fame leads to an even worse level of competition and the strong possibility of rejection by those who one has courted and in whom one has conferred strong psychological power.
Elevates, Raises One Up, More Than Human, *More Real* Fame makes one bigger than life through magnifying one's image out of proportion; fame confers a reality that many feel they lack.	*Less Real*	When they finally achieve fame, many discover that their feeling of *unreality* has only increased; the audience truly only cares about the role the celebrity is playing and how it satisfies the audience's needs.
Confers *Freedom From Death*, From Having to Change Fame promises the ultimate reward of living forever in the memories of people.	Increases One's *Vulnerability*, Ultimate Boundary Warping	Fame draws forth psychopaths who identify so closely with the famous that they use them (celebrities) to fill up their (the psychopaths') psychic holes; when the psychopaths feel that the celebrity in whom they have entrusted themselves for completion has let them down, assassination is often the payment; the psychopathic fans cannot draw a line between themselves and those who they identify with.

TABLE 2

The Ledger Sheet of Fame (Cont'd.)

The Presumed Benefits of Fame		The Potential Costs of Fame	
Erases the Gap, Greater Congruity	Fame erases the gap between the value the person puts on himself and the value the public does:	*Enlarges* the Gap	The gap can never be removed as long as it is dependent on others; the gap is inside the person, not outside.
The *Ultimate End State* of Arrival, Having Made It	Fame is the ultimate pinnacle.	*Dynamic*, It Never Ends	Each project of feeling of success has to be topped for the feeling is that one is either continually moving upwards or one is going straight down; self-destruction is the way out of this endless trap; the feeling is that if one can make oneself then one can unmake oneself through self-destruction.

Adapted from Braudy, *The Frenzy of Renown*.[18]

had hit bottom and was relegated...to reading 43-second news updates, all the while withdrawing into...the "pathology of stardom."

Savitch's ever-shrinking professional world was dominated by a core of doting personal attendants—groomers, wardrobe helpers and secretaries—who...formed a "warm, unthreatening, loyal wall between her and the increasingly hostile world outside."

She got so weirded out on cocaine, her addiction was in full [swing]....By 1980, she was snorting from morning till night. She was so paranoid by that time that sometimes she wouldn't go to work. But this was someone who had more than a drug problem. She had a severe personality disorder. Right before she died, she was in dreadful physical shape. Her weight was low, her hair and nails were ragged, she had ulcerated sores from the drugs and her hands were shaking."[19]

There is another aspect to the dark side of celebrityhood that must be mentioned. It is known from recent studies that the suicide rate in the general population goes up when a famous celebrity commits suicide.[20] What's truly important is that the suicide rate in the general population varies significantly depending upon the "sector" from which the celebrity comes, and seems to be greatest when the celebrity in question comes from the entertainment sector. In other words, *the dark side of the celebrity industry is our dark side as well*.

Concluding Remarks: The Emasculation and Irrelevancy of Ethics

That we are highly critical of celebrityhood and unreality should not be interpreted that we are critical of entertainment and celebrityhood in general. If we are critical, it is only of the worst excesses that both are capable of. For instance, the general shielding of modern art and entertainment (unreality in general) from truth and criticism makes it possible for the authors of *High Visibility* to tout the creation and marketing of a porno queen such as Seka on the same level as the creation of a legitimate celebrity. The suppression of criticism and truth, the suspension of ethics, the self-sealing character of entertainment so that it becomes a universe of discourse subject only to its own rules—all these are merely some of the mechanisms of unreality that underlie some of the worst aspects of the manufacturing of celebrities. We quote:

> Seka is the uncontested leader of the pornographic movie sector. Her earnings top those of all competitors in her sector: "$100,000 or so for a film, $15,000 for a one-day film appearance, 'four figures' for a one-day live appearance, $60 for a five-minute phone conversation." She even gets $14.95 for a pair of her used underwear. Most importantly, Seka is a celebrity made by transformation. Under the guidance of her mentor/manager she undertook a physical regimen involving diet, four and one-half hours of daily exercise, diction and drama lessons, and improvements in her posture, appearance, and deportment. With her trademark platinum locks, she is instantly recognizable. Even her invented name is memorable. It's short and exotic. Her competition, X-rated performers Marilyn Chambers and Sylvia Crystal [sic]—while still making films—cannot match the sophistication of Seka's approach to marketing.[21]

It would be wrong to conclude that, as a result of the industrialization of celebrities that is so rampant in our society, all mystery has vanished from the scene. Some sense of mystery is always necessary to the successful creation of celebrities and their appeal to the masses. All art and artists constantly flirt on the borderline between heightening mystery and reducing it. A telling point, however, is that in our times what passes for art can only survive and flourish on the basis of the most *minimal* mystery. A recent article in *Time* entitled, "Yuppie Lit: Publicize Or Perish," captures perfectly the mood of our era:

> Janowitz, like her friend the late Andy Warhol, understands that people will look at anything rather than nothing: art-like artifacts if there is no art, and book-like objects if there is no literature.

Self-promotion and celebrity may not bring down Western Civilization, though they have harmed writers with considerably more to show and say than Janowitz and other young bright lights of the moment. F. Scott Fitzgerald paid the price of fame, but, says the critic and memoirist Alfred Kazin, "He wanted to be the best. I don't hear anyone talking of being the best today. Books are now made as movies are. There is no belief that a book has a long life. Writers have abandoned the idea of making a masterpiece. Now they are Hollywood venture capitalists and accomplices in all that is happening."

That includes a premium on visual effects and an emphasis on rudimentary characterization, both earmarks of immature writing and feature films, where the bulk of the audience is under 25. Only the future can tell which young writers will be ready to bleed for their art and which will continue to write with ice cold Perrier in their veins.

The suppression of external criticisms and ethical concerns by *any* industry is damaging to the moral health, the values, of a democratic society. What after all can be the state of a society and a culture that deludes itself into believing that its marketing technologies are morally neutral so that they can be applied without harm equally to the promotion and development of porno queens, presidential candidates, business leaders, and comic entertainers?

> *The truth is that very few people care. The reason is that the confusing of real life and "role" life is now a fixture of business and politics as much as entertainment. It is a deliberate strategy to make celebrities knowable to their publics as friends, while taking advantage of the audience's desire to see traditional story lines embodied in celebrities' real lives as well as in their public, media-delivered "performance" lives* [italics ours]. Celebrities in old Hollywood had a perfect system for taking advantage of the power of associating themselves with images: the fictional tales they enacted in their films, and the gossip columnists' delivery of the images of their private lives to large publics. Today, the highly visible in every sector are marketing the images they supposedly live. Is Federal Reserve Chairman Paul Volcker *really* the "second most powerful person in America"? Is author Erica Jong *always* so open and vulnerable? Does actress Goldie Hawn *never* get depressed? Who are these people?[22]

To answer our own question, then, as to what the fate of any society can be that embodies such values: it must experience a marked if not near epidemic increase in the negative consequences associated with fame before it will recognize its follies. We should expect that not just individual celebrities will experience a greater sense of entrapment, of bigger holes in their personalities, of greater feelings of rejection, or being less real, of greater vulnerability, of a wider gap between the values they put on themselves and what society places on them, of being on a never-ending treadmill. No, we should expect that more of us will experience these very same symptoms. We should expect that societies that are hooked on massive amounts of unreality in order for them to function will experience greater degrees of addiction to a wide variety of deadly opiates.

6. The Culture of Unreality
Historical Roots

For forty-three years, whenever anyone discussed the difficult process of combining animation with live action in movies, the model of success has been the scene in *Anchors Aweigh* where Gene Kelly does a bouncy dance with Jerry the Mouse.

From today on, the model will be *Who Framed Roger Rabbit?* Pick your scene.

"Roger Rabbit," the collaborative brainchild of film director Robert Zemeckis and animation genius Richard Williams, displays the most inventive, effective integration of animation and live action ever attempted.

Zemeckis and Williams discovered what they really disliked were the unwritten rules governing the blending of animation and live action: don't move the live action camera, and keep physical interaction between the live actors and the cartoon characters to a minimum. The more camera movement, the more difficult it is for artists to match their drawings to the action. The more interaction, the more difficult it is to make the interaction seem real.

—Charles Solomon, "Live Action and Animation Join Forces With Human Genius and High Tech," Calendar Section, *Los Angeles Times*, June 22, 1988, pp. 1, 8.

What's amazing about *Who Framed Roger Rabbit?* ...a sort of inked-in *film noir* with outrageous sight gags, is how quickly we begin to accept the miracle in front of our eyes...

Within ten more minutes, we have accepted human criss-crossing into Roger's world, the second-class, metaphoric world of the Toons—animated stars, contract players and bit actors who work at Hollywood's Maroon Studios in 1947. We believe that when a seedy gumshoe, Eddie Valiant (Bob Hoskins), walks onto the Maroon lot he has to squeeze by a tutu-ed Toon hippo on the stairs and avoid getting his feet wet as a squad of brooms from *Fantasia* scrub down a sound stage. (Hoskins must have a cast-iron imagination to carry off this delicately calibrated interraction with every size and variety of Toon, from a rabbit in his bed, to an eight-foot gorilla looming menacingly over his shoulder, to a seductress with Gloria Grahame's mouth and Jayne Mansfield's silhouette.)

—Sheila Benson, "The Animated Wonders of 'Roger Rabbit,' Movie Review: Feverishly Inventive Mix of Actors, Cartoon Characters," Calendar Section, *Los Angeles Times*, June 22, 1988, p. 9.

In the past three chapters, we have been exploring the general nature of unreality: what it is, how it is produced, and, to a certain extent, why it is produced, i.e., the human needs and purposes it satisfies. In the next two chapters, we'd like to examine in greater detail the deeper needs and human purposes that unreality serves. We will be exploring at the same time a deeper set of mechanisms that are responsible for the production of unreality.

It is important to look at these additional factors since the increased complexity of the world that we treated in Chapter Two is not the complete story of our general fascination with unreality. Even if the world itself had not increased greatly in complexity, our contention would still be that there are other forces locked up inside U.S. culture and the human mind in general that predisposes us to unreality. It is important to explore these additional factors if we are to avoid the trap of getting caught in quick fix, band-aid solutions so that in our last chapter we can form a better assessment of what one can do to reverse our preoccupation with unreality.

The constant search for quick fix solutions is itself one of the principal features of U.S. culture. Quick fix solutions, however, nearly always perpetuate the problems they are intended to solve, and often make them even worse.

Everything which humans create is a testimony to their nature. We should expect therefore that the kinds of unreality people create are a reflection among other things of the kinds of mind humans possess and the history and the general culture of the particular society in which they are situated. Some features of unreality should therefore be the same for all cultures while others should be unique to a particular culture.

In this chapter, we want to examine five important features in particular of the human mind and/or U.S. culture that contribute to our society's special susceptibility and extreme fondness for unreality. They are:

— the cognitive structure of the human mind;
— its archetypal structure;
— those particular features of American society that have especially predisposed us to adopt technological solutions to all our problems;
— our fondness for bigness; and
— the narcissism that is particularly rampant in American culture.

The Cognitive Structure of the Human Mind

In recent years, what we have learned about the cognitive structure of the human mind helps us to understand why many of the mechanisms that were designed and/or evolved for man's survival (e.g., the ability to notice out of the corner of one's eye what appears to be a tiger fleeting by) are especially ripe for exploitation by the mechanisms of unreality that we have identified previously.[1] Thus, for example, consider some of the prime features of TV: the frenetic, machine-gun-like bursts of noise that emanates from it 24 hours a day; the radical shifts and breakups between scenes; the frequent uses of hi-tech graphics and bizarre sounds, colors, and dress to hold the attention of viewers for no more than 15 to 20 seconds. These features of TV and more pioneered by the so-called "greats" of the medium who discovered/invented them turn out on examination to be no more than exploitation of the remnant structure of our minds left over from early evolution.

Three features in particular of the human mind contribute especially to our fondness for unreality:

1. *What Have You Done for Me Lately?*
   We are extremely sensitive to recent information; emotional upsets like bad feelings last for a while, then are forgiven. Terrible disasters like an air crash force attention on airliners for a while; all sorts of reforms are initiated and then the spotlight goes away.

2. *Don't Call Me Unless Anything New and Exciting Happens.*
   We are interested only in "the news," the sudden appearance of something unknown. Unexpected or extraordinary events seem to have fast access to consciousness, while an unchanging background noise, a constant weight, or a chronic problem soon gets shunted into the background. It is easy to raise money for emergencies, like the few victims of a well publicized disaster; it's much more difficult to raise money for the many victims of continuous malnutrition. We respond quickly to scarcity and danger. Gradual changes in the world go unnoted while sharp changes are immediately seized on by the mind.

3. *Get to the point!*
   The mental system determines the meaning of any event, its relevance to the person. In the process, it throws out almost all the information that reaches us. Of the billions of leaves you saw last summer, how many do you remember? A flash of red crossing your view may mean that your wife has driven home in a red car, but you hardly notice the visual stimulus, just its meaning. A siren is frightening because it *means* that the police want you to stop.[2]

Our minds are set up to simplify, to bring order to a world that often is as chaotic as it appears. To do this we not only throw out a great deal of information that is presented to us but we lock in, long after they have seemed to retain their usefulness or validity, older patterns and pieces of information. These features alone help to explain some of the other "great" discoveries of the entertainment/celebrity industry. The industry capitalizes on our great need for simplifying patterns by exploiting it fully. It indulges in simplification overkill. It realizes that few people who can make it as celebrities can have complex or multiple story lines and still survive in the public's consciousness. Complexity leads to a loss of clear-cut identity. That's why a clear-cut, single and simple, unambiguous story line, especially one that ideally can be maintained indefinitely, is so important:

> ...We probably are the ultimate in simplemindedness about others. We select only a few items about each person to go into the fast path judgments, as we do for everything else. We try to make them more stable than they are. We may quickly judge someone, for instance, as a prototypical kindly old man and then try to fit his actions into the "correct" category. Or, more likely, we select a few key features that go along with being, for instance, kindly and restrict our observation to them, largely *in the same situation*, over time. Because behavior *is* consistent in the same situation over time, we can maintain our coherent perception ("He is honest"; "She is conscientious") and simply ignore many other situations and behavior of that person.[3]

Archetypal Engineering[4]

The stereotyping of people, for instance "the kindly old man" noted above, is but a tiny example of a more general phenomenon that explains at a much deeper level our need for unreality. This more general phenomenon is that of archetypes.[5]

Archetypes constitute the deepest and most symbolic aspects of the mind that humans use to give order to their world. Most often observed in dreams in the form of mythological characters, they are even more readily seen through an analysis of comparative world mythology, legends, fairy tales, religion and so on. The more that one examines the great diversity of world cultures, the more one finds that at a symbolic level there is an astonishing amount of agreement between various archetypal images. People may disagree and fight one another by day but at night they show the most profound similarity in their dreams and myths. Their agreement is too strong to be produced by chance alone. It is therefore attributed to a similarity of the human psyche at the deepest layers of the unconscious. These similar appearing symbolic images are termed archetypes.

At the most elemental level, archetypes help people develop an emotionally satisfying picture of the world. The world is so terrifying both to the primitive and to the child that they need some way of coping with it and of organizing it. They cannot use the techniques available to the adult. They cannot psychologically distance themselves enough to give a disinterested, rational, or scientific picture of the world. Since the child and the primitive project their inner fears out onto the external world, little wonder that some of the most universal and potent archetypal images are the strangest looking demons—half-human/half-animal creatures. (Recall the half-human/half-machine creatures that inhabit the Saturday morning kids' shows and music videos.) Through archetypes we thus have the opportunity to witness from precisely where in the human psyche such images originate and what purposes they serve.

The blurring of the shapes between men and animals is a familiar archetypal theme. Blurring represents a primitive stage in the evolution of the human mind—the stage where people are not yet able to differentiate the animal instincts that emanate from within them from those of the animals that they confront in the outer world. The Saturday morning kids' shows thus exploit the very same primitive lack of differentiation that kids have between their animal instincts and those of the images that they see on the screen.

Every aspect of a person's existence is capable of being turned into an archetypal symbol, image, or character. Thus, there exists an archetypal mythological character for every part of a person's psyche and social nature:

> Archetypes include such prototypal [basic human] experiences as food gathering, elimination, fertility, father, mother, authority, self, femininity, goddess, eternity, childhood, circle, square, devil (evil), god (good), maleness, and sleep. If we look at the core essence of a symbol...we will find evidence for archetypal influences.
>
> Since all men have created some form of religion no matter where they sprang up, religion should provide us with residues of concrete deposits of archetypal action. Christ and The Buddha symbolize some essence of archetypal deposit for us, since they are the religious representative of our era.[6]

There are archetypes corresponding to every authority figure, to every condition of chance or uncertainty, war, death, occupation, and so on. The eminent psychoanalyst Bruno Bettelheim has put it well in explaining the hold that fairy tales have on the mind of the child and hence the need that we have for archetypes:

> Contrary to what takes place in modern children's stories in fairy tales evil is as omnipresent as virtue. In practically every fairy tale good and evil are given body in the form of some figures and their actions, as good and evil, are omnipresent in life and the properties for both are present in every man. It is this duality which poses the moral problem and requires the struggle to solve it....
>
> The figures in fairy tales are not ambivalent—not good and bad at the same time, as we all are in reality. But since polarization dominates the child's mind, it also dominates fairy tales. A person is either good or bad, nothing in between...One parent is all good, the other evil...Presenting the polarities of character permits the child to comprehend easily the differences between the two, which he could not do as readily were the figures drawn more true to life, with all the complexities that characterize real people. Ambiguities must wait until a relatively firm personality has been established on the basis of positive identifications.

Then the child has a basis for understanding that there are great differences between people, and that therefore one has to make choices about who one wants to be. This basic decision, on which all later personality developments will build, is facilitated by the polarizations of the fairy tale.[7]

It would be a serious mistake to think that such raw images and projections are absent from the thoughts of adults. It is undoubtedly true that the historical context of the vast majority of archetypes that humans have experienced throughout the ages is by now so far removed from our direct experience and daily lives that ancient traditional forms have little contemporary meaning for us. At best, they appear bizarre, as if from another planet. At worst, they seem to degenerate hopelessly into mysticism. And yet, this is precisely the attitude we must avoid.

Over the last few years, a whole series of computer games has evolved that allows players to test their skills in competition against a set of formidable opponents, i.e., the characters that compose the games. These games show as well that unreality is not confined merely to TV but rather has spread throughout nearly every feature of our society. The ads for these "games" make perfectly clear the archetypal nature of the opponents that are built into them. The ads portray, in the slickest and glossiest of terms (the artwork that accompanies the games), the most diverse pantheon of mythological characters that one can do battle against. Not only are there mythological characters— Minotaurs and half-human/half-animal creatures—but the men and the women that appear in the games are themselves larger than life in every physical feature. They make the characters in *Conan the Barbarian* look tame by comparison.

Irony of ironies: The computer, perhaps *the* modern archetype of impersonal, cold, calculating science and technology, has itself become the prime projective dumping ground of humanity's inner psyche. This conclusion becomes all the more striking and powerful when one realizes that one has very little reason to think that the designers of these games had any conscious appreciation of the fact they were projecting their internal archetypes onto their computerized creations.

One of the best if not most striking examples of these games is *Wizardry*. A recent article in the computer magazine *Softline* puts it as follows:

> *Wizardry* is a game apart from others of its genre. Its success probably rests on its unique abilities: no other game allows as much flexibility in building your own characters, designating strengths and weaknesses that have clear effects; and more important, no other game allows you to take a group of characters, up to six at a time, into [a] dungeon, where they interact and work together to overcome monsters and obstacles. Characters can trade gold and equipment freely, cast beneficial spells on each other, and change position in the expedition to benefit all. Or they can run from all monsters; if one runs, all run.[8]

Robert Woodhead, one of the game's designers and one of the very few with a background in psychology—and hence some insight into the popularity of his own creation—freely acknowledges that *Wizardry* is a "projective game." That is, "people tend to put their personalities in the characters they invent":

> The world of *Wizardry* can be populated with characters of different races—dwarf, elf, gnome, hobbit, human—and different classes starting as [sorcerers], priests, fighters, or thieves; characters can earn the right to become samurai, bishops, and lords. The dungeon has ten levels to conquer and there are numerous personal levels through which your characters progress as they gain experience and strengthen their attributes. You can create as many as twenty characters per [computer program], any six of which you can gather in the tavern to send on an expedition to the maze. Together your band fights monsters, searches for treasures, or has a good old time at the inn.[9]

As those who have played *Wizardry* testify in their own words, it is more than "just a game." The characters one creates are part of one's self. Hence, when one of the characters dies, it is like having a part of oneself die as well.

Verbatim quotes from those who have played the game are revealing of the hold that such "games" have on the psyche:

> It sure helps to relax a person after a hard day at work. That troll does look like my boss; sometimes I submerge myslef in my characters, I lose almost all sense of my own identity. I once played for three days straight without coming up out of the game. When my party was finally devastated, I almost broke down into tears; I'd liken *Wizardry* to a fantasized system of personnel management. As the manager of a small group of individuals...you must manipulate the members' performance against the "competition" so that they achieve a certain goal. In *Wizardry*, as in real life, the goal can be mere survival, or the quest for power, or, over the long haul, the pot of gold.[10]

Perhaps the most interesting and potentially important use of such games is in the field of child psychotherapy. This application also shows that we are not talking about the complete abandonment or nondevelopment of such techniques at all, but rather, only more reflective consideration given to their potentially socially productive use. An accepted psychotherapeutic technique of working with children, who cannot verbalize their inner emotional states as well as adults, is that of play therapy. What children play with and how they do offer a window into their inner world. Thus, for instance, if a certain doll represents a parent and it is treated in a rough manner, then one gets a glimpse from the child of what's going on inside him/her in relationship to a parent. Because *Wizardry* allows one to create a number of characters and to project onto them characteristics in which one may be deficient, there is the opportunity for an outsider to observe those issues one is wrestling with psychologically. This holds no less true for adults than it does for children.

How ironic that a machine which has come to symbolize the epitome of humanity's impersonal, calculating abilities carried to the highest levels of scientific and technological development should come to serve as a prime vehicle for the observation of the psyche. It seems no matter what humanity attempts, it is doomed to observe its archetypal nature staring back at it. Archetypes are not dead, as by definition they could never be. They just crop up in the strangest of places. They are alive—whether they are "well" is another matter—and functioning on the computer as are all the other mechanisms we have explored in this book. Howver, if this is the case, then it explains the deep fascination and appeal that such "games" have for "kids" of all ages. No wonder it is so easy to get hooked on video and computer games. The addicting quality is within all of us. As a result, it is impossible to ban all such games. They merely come back in other forms. If there is a serious debate that deserves to be held, it should be over the *forms* of archetypes that are acceptable, not their ultimate restriction. If the games are archetypal, then total restriction is mortally impossible. Even more fundamental is the question of responsibility for the design of archetypes on computers. What does one do? Appoint a Federal commission for the study and protection of archetypes? To whom or what does one turn in society for the legitimate and responsible use of the deepest, most fundamental components of the human mind?

If archetypes have made a new and fundamental link with the computer as we believe, then we can make some important, if not disturbing, predictions. One of the most significant occurrences, we believe, is the inevitable intrusion of archetypal games in large theme parks, like Disneyland and Walt Disney World. It is only a small step from archetypes contained within a computer program and projected onto a TV screen to exotic rides (better yet, "experiences") where one can play with archetypes in the form of robots. The technology that is capable of doing one can ultimately do the other. Whether because it can be done it should be done is of course the fundamental dilemma.

Recently, Norwegian psychologist Paul Moxnes[11] has used the concept of archetypes to develop an intriguing framework that helps explain the basis for some of the most central figures that appear repeatedly in human culture, from the Bible through contemporary soap operas. Moxnes starts with the characters that compose the basic nuclear family, i.e., father, mother, son, and daughter. He then notes that every one of these basic characters has both a bad and a good side. He further observes that archetypes tend to split these good and bad aspects into sharply divergent characters so that the good father assumes in general a very different archetypal nature and character structure than that of the bad father. When all of the nuclear family characteristics are polarized, or split into their good and bad opposites, the following result:

> The Good Father becomes God.
> The Bad Father becomes the Devil.
> The Good Mother, the Queen.
> The Bad Mother, the Witch
> The Good Son, the Crown Prince
> The Bad Son, the Black Sheep
> The Good Daughter, the Princess
> and finally,
> the Bad Daughter, the Whore

Moxnes also feels that there are secondary characters that also come into play. These are known as the "helpers" to the primary characters. As before, they are split into good and bad archetypes:

> The Good Slave/Servant becomes the Faithful Servant
> The Bad Slave/Servant becomes the Disloyal Servant
> The Good Wiseman/Shaman becomes known as the Doctor
> The Bad Wiseman/Shaman becomes known as the False Prophet

Finally, Moxnes says that there are two additional characters whose purpose is to help the characters transform themselves. Again, these as well are split into good and bad archetypal characters:

> The Good Winner/Hero becomes Cinderella
> The Bad Winner/Hero takes on a form of for example the "Godfather"

The Good Loser abdicates and withdraws from power
The Bad Loser must be removed or killed

Given this system of archetypes, Moxnes uses them to construct Table 1 which shows how they have appeared in various books and media from the Bible to popular soap operas of the day such as *Dynasty*.

The whole field of archetypal psychology gives a new and frightening interpretation of many of the issues discussed with regard to the celebrity industry in the last chapter. Consider for example the following quote from *High Visibility*:

> To be marketed successfully, *individuals need to gain control of their images* [italics ours], making decisions based on a thorough understanding of all aspects of how marketing operates in the celebrity industry. The person trying to execute a high visibility plan needs to understand not just the tricks of projecting the right images, but how the best images are determined and how they can be produced.[12]

What the authors of *High Visibility* apparently have no feeling for whatsoever is the truly explosive forces of the human personaltiy with which they are playing. There is no doubt that individuals can delude themselves into thinking that they can choose rationally at the conscious level "the images" they wish to project. What such people almost always fail to realize is that there is a due to be paid to the devil. The reason why one is bargaining with the devil is that although archetypes are generally split by their nature into polar opposites, the splitting is never perfect or complete. In terms of the last chapter where we presented a ledger sheet of the presumed benefits versus the cost of fame, one can never guarantee that one will reap only the benefits without thereby incurring the terrible costs to be paid to fame.

In-depth studies of archetypal psychology reveal an astounding fact. If archetypes demonstrate that there is a personalized content to our minds no matter how far down we descend into its structure, then one of the most astounding properties of archetypes is that all of them are

TABLE 1

ARCHETYPAL ROLES IN FOUR DIFFERENT
CULTURAL FIELDS

Archetypal Characters		Fairy Tales	Bible	Greek Mythology	"Dynasty"
Father	Good	King	God	Zeus	Blake
	Bad	Troll/Beast	Devil	(Hades)	Colby/Rinewood
Mother	Good	Queen	Madonna/Maria	Hera	Krystal
	Bad	Witch	?	(Persephone)	Alexis
Son	Good	Crown Prince	Jesus	Apollo	Jeff
	Bad	Black Sheep	Lost Son	Ares	Steven
Daughter	Good	Princess/Virgin	Virgin Mary	Atene	Fallon/Claudia
	Bad	Whore	Maria Magdalena	(Aphrodite)	Sammy-Jo
Slave/Servant		Courtier	Martha	Hermes	Joseph
Wiseman/Doctor		Old Man/Animal	Jesus/Lucas	Aesculapius	Doctor Toscani
Winner/Hero		Ash Lad	Jesus	Hercules	Krystal/Adam
Loser		Anonymous	Anonymous	(Prometheus)	Anonymous

contained within one another. The overlap and spillover between them is tremendous. Thus, for example, the Good Father may be on its surface primarily beneficent. But in order to round out its character, like that of all human beings, there is always an element of the Bad Father present in the Good Father as well, and vice versa.

It turns out that no matter how pure or one sided we attempt to make archetypal images, we can never exclude something of its opposite from intruding if only for purposes of roundness, completion, or balance. Thus, *High Visibility* glosses over too quickly because it is either unaware or chooses not to become aware of the dangers in "choosing our images." It is thus oblivious to the extreme dangers with which one is playing. The dangers come out in the form of suicide, depression, drug addiction, failed marriages, and the like. The reason is that choosing an image and living it are often two very different things particularly when the image that is chosen consciously may go deeply against the grain of the archetypes that naturally constitute the deeper layers of the psyche of a human being one is tampering with.

One could cite hundreds of cases from the "true confessions" of fallen stars, for as we noted in the previous chapter, the "confessions" themselves are all part of the scripted story line of being a celebrity. For instance, Margaux Hemingway's "story" of her rise and fall and possible rise again appears appropriately enough in *People*, a magazine that is the very epitome of scripted lives:

> For me, beccoming a celebrity was like being in the eye of a hurricane. Suddenly I was an international cover girl. Everybody was lapping up my Hemingwayness. They wanted to rub elbows with me or brush up against me. As a child I had seen Lauren Hutton on a magazine cover, and I thought that the fast lane was as exhilarating as racing down a mountain on skis. I was meeting famous people and constantly traveling all over the world. I remember being really poor until I got my first $250,000 check from Faberge. That was pretty nice; I put it in the bank and from that moment on there seemed to be a lot of champagne and limousines in my life. Being on the cover of *Time* was

another high for me. I lost my passport in Spain, and that
cover got me through customs.

It sounds glamorous, and it was. I was having a lot of fun.
But I was also very naive when I came on the scene. I
genuinely thought that people liked me for myself—for my
humor and good qualities. I never expected to meet so
many professional leeches.[13]

The study of archetypal psychology reveals another
important consequence as well. If archetypes, no matter
how one-sided they appear on their surface, contain nonetheless a strong ingredient of their opposite which can
burst forth unexpectedly at any time—indeed all the more
when one thinks that one can reap only the positive
aspects—then this means that at the most fundamental
layers of the human personality Boundary Warping is
present. In fact, archetypal psychology gives us insight into
why Boundary Warping is so fundamental a characteristic
of the human condition. No matter how deep one pene-
trates into the human psyche, no matter what levels of
depth to which one descends, one finds a fundamental lack
of clarity and sharpness between the various aspects of the
human psyche and the problems and the issues with which
it is struggling. The point is that the Boundary Warping we
find in the media both consciously and unconsciously plays
on this fundamental Boundary Warping that is present at
the archetypal level. The deepest sources of Boundary
Warping, in other words, emanate from the human psyche
itself.

American Culture: The Roots of Amerian Unreality

As we have seen, those aspects of the mind that were
programmed by evolution for purposes of survival are
especially ripe for exploitation by the various forms and
mechanisms of unreality that we have identified. For
instance, TV takes advantage of the brain's special atten-
tiveness to recent events and particularly those which flit
across the visual span of the viewer with speed or height-
ened color. We are programmed by evolution to unreality's
special fondness for hyperactiveness. However, the brain's

receptiveness to fast moving stimuli is not sufficient in itself to account for America's special preoccupation with unreality. More than the workings of the brain alone are needed to account for the intensity with which Americans pursue unreality with a fever that approaches a national crusade. And indeed, to inveigh the phrase "national crusade" already implies that another part of the answer is to be found in American culture.

Hyperactivity is not only a deeply ingrained feature of American culture by virtue of the special fortitude of those who journeyed to the new land in order to settle it—it was a dire necessity for survival—but, as a result, it has become linked with other fundamental American values and beliefs. Americans have always believed deeply in material progress. The two words "material" and "progress" are virtually inseparable. Each implies the other in the context of the American experience. As the historian Jackson Lears has put it in his marvelous treatise on the Antimodernist movement which took place between the years 1880 to 1920 (1880, the rough founding date of the movement, is approximately halfway between the founding of the Republic and present times, thus serving to connect both our early history and present times):

> ...Americans who despised the steel magnate Andrew Carnegie would have echoed his claim in *Triumphant Democracy* (1886): "The old nations of the earth creep on at a snail's pace; the Republic thunders past with the rush of the express." Carnegie revealed the major foundation of the belief in progress: the idea that nations (like individuals) can never stand still. They must always be growing, changing, improving their material lot; life is a race to be won by the swiftest. Like the progressive faith itself, this notion was often left implicit. Yet its impact has been incalculable. It accounts for the relentless dynamism at the heart of capitalist development, spreading an obsessive need for change throughout modern culture. And for most educated and affluent Americans in the late 19th century, "change" meant "progress."[14]

Such progress we have learned was bought at a considerable price. To the uprooting and mass migration from farms and small country hamlets into the cities with their teeming slums and social problems on scales not experienced before, Americans reacted against what they experienced as the "unreality of the new social order." Removed from nature with its natural sounds, sights, and rhythms, Americans felt a great sense of uneasiness. They found the new factories with their vast management hierarchies and impersonal rules the very epitome of everything that was unnatural, unreal, stultifying, and suffocating. Men felt that they were in danger of becoming the very machines with which they worked and were charged with controlling. As we noted in Chapter One, in Thoreau's phrase we were in danger of becoming the tools of our tools. Lears has put it well:

> This sense of unreality has become part of the hidden agenda of modernization. Throughout the 20th century, recoil from the artificial, overcivilized qualities of modern existence has sparked a wide variety of quests for more intense experience, ranging from the fascist fascination with violence and death, to the cults of emotional spontaneity of avant-garde artists to popular therapies stressing instinctual liberation. Antimodern impulses, too, were rooted in longings to recapture an illusive "real life" in a culture evaporating into unreality.[15]

In reaction to the growing sense of unreality brought on by the difficult adjustment to the new realities of modern life, Americans of all social classes retreated to and engaged in a frenzy-like search for authentic experience. To accomplish this, they extolled the virtues of manual labor and, much as busy, tired executives do in our times, they developed elaborate home workshops where handicraft projects were pursued with a vengeance. As these projects petered out, as they must eventually, Americans pursued other strains of Antimodernism. The most fascinating were a precursor to the cults of Eastern mysticism that were to capture the attention of the nation's youth and disaffected during the Vietnam era. Turned off by the excessive rationalization of thought and habits that modern bourgeois society and the industrial factory system demanded, Americans, especially the educated and well-to-do—including many businessmen themselves—turned to earlier periods of world history where men were not suffocated and hemmed in by rational modes of thought. A special fascination for the medieval ages developed. The medieval mind was regarded as primitive and unspoiled. Americans saw in the primitization of the medieval intellect, if not indeed its total personality, the deep sense for passionate experience, the direct contact with intense human emotions that they had long ago abandoned for modern life with all its promises of security, progress, comfort, etc.

The results of these pursuits are extremely instructive for they illustrate what is most likely to be the outcome of the reactions, if any, of our time against the forms of unreality we are experiencing. *In every case, the reactions of the Antimodernists against the unreality of their times was to strengthen the very forces of unreality against which they were reacting. Not only did the forces of opposition not weaken that which they were in opposition to but they actually strengthened them.* The basic reason is critical for our understanding.

All of the forces that were mounted in opposition to the new world that was being created could not change that world. Americans believed too strongly, too deeply, in material progress that was the product of objective, technological forces to turn back against those forces. In the end, all that the Antimodernist movement accomplished by focusing in on inner subjective experiences that were denied expression or were not being attended to by modern science in the modern industrial system was merely to allow those feelings an outlet for their expression. And paradoxically, the expression and venting of such "subjective feelings" promoted therapeutic adjustment to the new world order that was being created. In the end, the expression of feelings accelerated the very forces they were being produced in opposititon to. On every front, therefore, what began as a widespread revolt *against* the forces of Modernism ended up intensifying and *speeding up* the success of those very forces. For ultimately, Americans could not sustain for prolonged periods of time the same intensity of belief in subjective experience as they could in material progress. Hence, there was no hope of muting the technological forces that were at work in American culture.

We may be worse off than our forefathers. We may have so atrophied our emotional lives in the intervening period that we know no other sources in which to invest our emotional experiences than in our technology or dangerous cults that promote fascist violence.

We are subject to an incredible paradox. In our age, some of the most intense emotional experiences of the great masses of people revolve around forms of unreality that are themselves the direct products of technology. Earlier regarded as one of the most potent forms of unreality, technology is now responsible for producing some of unreality's strongest forms.

Bigness as Narcissism

One of the things that is most interesting about various national cultures is how much similar sounding ideas differ between them. Consider for instance the idea of "more" which we examined in some depth in Chapter Two. We argued there that the predominant conception of more in American society is that of bigness. As a culture, we tend to believe—deeply—that in general "bigger is better." Given the size of the land we inherited plus the boundless energy of the people who settled it, this connotation is easily understandable. People are shaped more by their geography than they realize. With a rich, bountiful, and seemingly endless landscape, why shouldn't Americans have believed, and continue to believe, that progress like the land itself was both material as well as endless?

Contrast this with the Japanese, one of our prime allies as well as competitors in the new world economy. Japan is literally a tiny island. If geography shapes people, then the Japanese are a perfect example. The country not only is tiny but occupies a highly precarious existence. It totters precariously on the brink of existence. It is poor in natural resources. It exists in an extremely harsh climate zone. It is racked continually by large earthquakes. Is it any wonder therefore why the Japanese have a survival mentality?

Cultures that are conditioned by a survival mentality develop in general very different conceptions of the world. The Japanese conception of "more" reflects precisely this.

Writing in the *Atlantic Monthly*, the distinguished journalist James Fallows[16] examined the differences in the conceptions of "more" that exist between Japanese and Americans. For Americans, "more" not only is tied up with bigness but is also an expression of our general social system. Fallows' argument is that in America the social system basically exists to serve the consumer; in Japan, it is exactly the other way around—it exists to serve the producer. "More" in America means that the greater efficiencies that are supposed to result from bigger industrial processes should be passed on in the form of lower prices or savings to consumers. "More" in Japan does not have to do with bigness per se. It also has to do with greater efficiencies in Japan, although it has to do, fundamentally, with this: whatever savings or benefits are achieved are to be passed on to producers.

When a country exists literally at the brink of survival, perhaps the only way in which it can guarantee that survival is to insure the continued existence of its infrastructure. Thus, "more" in Japan is or means insurance for the social good or harmony of the country as a whole.

In America, "more" serves and promotes greater individualism; in Japan, it promotes greater social harmony. What greater differences could there be?

In America, bigness is a reflection or expression of our narcissism, our exaggerated tendencies towards grandiosity. Everything is big in America or it is literally nothing, insignificant. Bigness as an expression of our narcissism is one of the deepest wellsprings of our tendencies towards unreality. The narcissism we have leads to unreality—to the feeling that somehow Americans are entitled to be number one among the nations of the world at the expense of the rest of mankind.

America was born in narcissism, shaped by it from its earliest beginnings. The pilgrims on the way to America conceived that they were founding a City on a Hill, a nation that was to be a moral beacon to the rest of the world. No other nation either before or since has been founded upon such yearnings.[17] As a result, how dare the rest of the world not see things the way we do? For instance, Lyndon Johnson literally could not understand why the North Vietnamese would not stop fighting if we merely offered to build them one of the biggest hydroelectric plants in the world?

Our concept of "more" as bigness virtually gets in the way of reality, clouding our judgments on important matters, leading to bad decisions. Narcissism, in short, leads to less. Thus, for instance, when in Vietnam the use of smaller, slower prop airplanes would have been better suited to the terrain, or reality, of the situation, the U.S. Air Force chose instead to use the biggest, most advanced planes to conduct the war:

> ...Many planners were aware that strategic bombing would not work on North Vietnam, and that its use in the south, against the guerrillas, would strengthen the guerrillas instead of weakening them. Nonetheless, the huge B-52's were wheeled out because they were at the center of the Air Force's most important function, strategic bombing of the U.S.S.R. If the Air Force had not been allowed to use these machines, it feared that the strategic-bombing role might be downgraded after the war. For the same reason, it insisted on using its highest performance jets in the south, as a historian concluded, "despite studies indicating that slower propeller driven models would have been three times as accurate, from five to thirteen times less costly, but with roughly the same loss ratio." Because the Air Force is the most technologically oriented of the services, it was incapable of using less than its best, even though less than the best would have been better.[18]

Concluding Remarks

Unreality must be regarded as the ultimate therapy of our age. But what a strange therapy it is! If it is good, then it is bad.

Unreality is at once both its own disease and treatment. However debatable its effectiveness is, it is a treatment in that it promotes adjustment to a reality no one can fully comprehend. Hence, no one can fully judge the curative powers of a treatment when the disease itself is not fully known.

It is a disease in that it is the unhealthy side of a reality that is badly in need of treatment. In this sense, unreality is best regarded as a narcotic. While each dose "cures" the pain of withdrawal or abuse from previous injections, it further strengthens the disease.

Unreality may thus provide a respite however brief from reality and in this sense promote therapeutic adjustment to the world. But it is not a true or effective cure. For a truly effective cure would remove the conditions promoting the disease in the first place. But again, isn't this all akin to the unreality on which the dope addict lives?

The history of unreality in this century alone presents a fascinating series of twists and contrasts.[19] It shows the successive stages through which the concept has developed. It shows that we are dealing clearly with a concept that is anything but simple or fixed. What is considered unreal for one time period is real for another, and vice versa. In other words, the unreality of one age becomes the reality of another.

In the beginning of this century, nature was considered real. The bureaucratic, overly rationalized world of the big industrial factory system was considered the unreality against which the Antimodernism movement was directed. As this century draws to a close, global interconnectedness is the new reality against which the varieties of unreality that we have discussed earlier are directed.

There is a fundamental difference between the two, however. Both the reality as well as the unreality of today are heavily technology based. Technology not only serves both but is a fundamental constituent of both, and it allows nearly simultaneous transmission of images and ideas in both realms. In the one, reality, technology so speeds up the transmission of ideas and events that it not only makes possible their beneficial results but it accelerates as well the resulting breakdown in coherence through the multiplication of crises and paradoxes that we discussed in Chapter Two. In the other, unreality, technology also speeds up the breakdown and/or irrelevancy of coherence through the overload of sensual images that are nearly completely devoid of any intellectual or cognitive content. In either case, we experience an attack on our sensibilities. We feel desperately the loss of any overall guiding framework to make sense of a world seemingly gone mad.

7. The Heroless, Leaderless Society

Contemporary Roots[1]

Many Americans are still hoping for the emergence of an old-style, dynamic "great leader." Yet electronic media of communication are making it almost impossible to find one. There is no lack of potential leaders, but rather an overabundance of information about them. The great leader image depends on mystification and careful management of public impressions. Through television, we see too much of our politicians, and they are losing control of their images and performances. As a result, our political leaders are being stripped of their aura and are being brought closer to the level of the average person.

...Michael Novak suggests in *Choosing Our King* that there is only paradox and futility in attempting to ignore images in favor of "reality." George McGovern..."ran for office as a man of candor, a politician unlike other politicians, a person unconcerned about image. *That* was his image." Novak argues that it is impossible for a politican to avoid having an image. "A candidate has only limited exposure; he must reach over 200,000,000 citizens; no one can look into his soul." Further, notes Novak, there is naivete and hypocrisy in pretending not to depend on image. Public office is "liturgical" in nature. An official does not act, should not act, is not expected to act solely in his or her private *persona*. He or she acts chiefly, and perhaps solely, as a public officer, representative of the people, in a role marked out by law and tradition."

—Joshua Meyrowitz, *No Sense of Place, The Impact of Electronic Media on Social Behavior*, New York: Oxford University Press, 1985, pp. 270, 278.

...The center of gravity...of the realm of mystery and danger has definitely shifted. For the primitive hunting peoples of those remotest human milleniums when the saber-toothed tiger, the mammoth, and the lesser presences of the animal kingdom were the primary manifestations of what was alien—the source at once of danger, and of sustinence—the great human problem was to become linked psychologically to the task of sharing the wilderness with these beings. An unconscious identification took place, and this was finally rendered conscious in the half-human, half-animal figures of the mythological totem-ancestors. The animals became the tutors of humanity. Through acts of literal imitation—such as today appear only on the children's playground (or in the madhouse)—an effective anihilation of the human ego was accomplished and society achieved a cohesive organization. Similarly, the tribes supporting themselves on plant-food became cathected to the plant; the life-rituals of planting and reaping were identified with those of human procreation, birth, and progress to maturity. Both the plant and the animal worlds, however, were in the end brought under social control. Whereupon the great field of instructive wonder shifted—to the skies—and mankind enacted the great pantomime of the sacred moon-king, the sacred sun-king, the hieratic, planetary state, and the symbolic festivals of the world-regulating spheres.

Today all of these mysteries have lost their force; their symbols no longer interest our psyche. The notion of a cosmic law, which all existence serves and to which man himself must bend, has long since passed through the preliminary mystical stages represented in the old astrology, and is now simply accepted in mechanical terms as a matter of course. The dissent of the Occidental sciences

from the heavens to the earth (from 17th-century astron-
omy to 19th-century biology), and their concentration
today, at last, on man himself (in 20th-century anthropology and psychology), mark the path of a prodigious trans-
fer of a focal point of human wonder. Not the animal
world, not the plant world, not the miracle of the spheres,
but man himself is now the crucial mystery. Man is that
alien presence with whom the forces of egoism must come
to terms, through whom the ego is to be crucified and
resurrected, and in whose image society is to be reformed.

—Joseph Campbell, *The Hero With 1000 Faces,* Bollingen
Series, Princeton University Press, 1968, pp. 390-391.

In the last chapter we argued that unreality arises because
of a multitude of factors and considerations. It does not do
so solely in response to the increased complexity of the
outside world. Social and cultural forces are as much
responsible for the rise and perpetuation of unreality as
are technical and environmental forces.

We want to continue this line of thought in this chapter.
We want to argue that we have killed off—literally, in some
cases—the conditions that make it possible for heroes to
emerge, to lead, to sustain, to nourish us. We want to argue
that not only have the old gods, myths, religions, and
symbols lost much, if not most, of their past power in
modern society, but that we are sorely lacking in replace-
ments. The old gods and myths no longer sustain us
because they are no longer deeply embedded in the
everyday lives of people. Further, society's present idols
(celebrities) no longer are worthy of the role and the title
"heroes," let alone "gods," because the modern process of
the deliberate manufacturing of pseudo heroes is at complete variance with the one by which true heroes historically have arisen.

Eminent scholars of mythology, Joseph Campbell
among them, have identified clearly the distinct stages
through which the development of heroes proceeds. In his
pathbreaking book, *The Hero With 1000 Faces,*[2] Campbell
has shown that the myth of the hero (i.e., the process by
which it develops) is strikingly similar across the ages and

the most diverse of cultures. By implication, he shows why it is increasingly difficult for heroes to arise in today's world.

One of the first stages in the development of the hero is The Call to Adventure, i.e., the happenstance, event or circumstance that elevates the aspiring hero from his/or everyday life—or ordinary reality—into a new, totally unexpected reality that will test and develop the person, if he/she is successful in meeting certain challenges, into a genuine hero. One of the most crucial points is that the challenges the inspiring hero has to face and conquer cannot be entirely preplanned, manufactured, or staged. Part of the reason is that the challenges come from the aspirant's own unconscious, and represent the internal demons and terrors (archetypes) the aspirant has to conquer within himself/herself. They can no more be completely planned or staged than what one dreams at night can be willed. This is why the best heroes are shaped as much by external circumstances not fully under their control as they are by formal training and education.

A good part of the hero's adventure consists of his or her leaving the everyday world—making a clean break—to encounter a world of mystery. And the mystery is not merely "out there in the world" but is, to a good degree, deep inside one as well, i.e., in the unconscious, underworld of forces (archetypes) with which the aspirant is struggling. The battle, thus, is with the person himself/herself. But if so, how can the hero in today's world identify, let alone do battle with, his or her internal mysteries if they are constantly in the media spotlight? Where can potential aspirants go in modern societies to get away sufficiently from ordinary reality in order to confront themselves? Notice that we are not talking about the phony mystification of pseudo celebrities or the deliberate withholding of public information by responsible officials. Rather, to develop, the hero needs to go off, to separate, to develop himself or herself so as to reenter society and possibly change everyday reality.

This only leads us to a further discussion of why heroes/leaders are rarer in contemporary society. The purpose then of this chapter is to explore other, less obvious facets of unreality by assessing the state of contemporary leadership in modern society.

Our discussion is intended to show that there is no doubt whatsoever that we have been and will continue to be highly successful in developing the technical means to produce characters and images. But this *manufacturing technology* and its end product should not be confused with the *social process* that it takes to produce genuine heroes/ leaders. *Technology* may be able to produce characters, but it is not able to produce *character*. The confusion, lack of understanding between these two is one of the prime characteristics of our culture.

Why has it become increasingly difficult to secure genuine heroes/leaders in contemporary America and what does this tell us further about unreality?

The Roots of the Heroless, Leaderless Society

Two hundred years ago, when the Founding Fathers gathered in Philadelphia to write the Constitution, America had a population of only three million, yet six world class leaders contributed to the making of that extraordinary document. Today, there are nearly 250 million Americans, and we have...Ollie North, the thinking man's Rambo. Clearly, if America is not to become a kind of Mega Banana Republic, we must do better.

Leaders come in every size, shape, and disposition, but they have in common the vision which is compelling to other people, and, by fully deploying themselves, the ability to make their vision manifest. They have, in other words, a passion for the promises of life. Washington, Jefferson, Adams, Hamilton, Franklin and Madison had that passion, as did Lincoln, John and Robert Kennedy and Martin Luther King. None of our current so-called leaders has it. Today, passion is out, and ambition is in.

As 18th century America was notable for its geniuses, and 19th century America for its freewheeling adventurers, entrepreneurs, inventors and scientists, 20th century America has been chiefly notable for its bureaucrats and managers. What those Philadelphia geniuses created, and their rowdy successors embellished, the organization men—in both government and business—have remade, or unmade.

Unlike either our Founding Fathers or the industrial titans, the managers of America's giant corporations and the bureaucrats, elected and appointed, who run the government have no gut stake in the enterprise and no vision. More often than not, they're mere hired guns, following the money. The end result is that unreality has become our general substitute for our lack of vision. Where once our psychological energy was invested, as Joseph Campbell has pointed out, in people, animals, plants, nature, and dreams, we invest it now in technology and pseudo heroes.

In the first decades of this century, as both business and government got bigger, they began to get in each other's way. The bureaucrats imposed rules and regulations on big business. Corporate managers countered by flooding Washington with lobbyists, and a new era began: America of, by and for special interests. A stalemate developed as bureaucrats and managers traded favors. Nothing much grows in a stalemate, of course, but managers and bureaucrats are less gardeners than mechanics—fonder of tinkering with the machinery than making it go.

There were ironies. As we noted in Chapter Two, having emerged from World War II as the richest and most powerful nation on earth, America had lost its edge by the mid-1970s. The much bruited American Century was suddenly the Japanese Century—in business anyway. It's anyone's guess whose century it is politically, but tiny nations, like Iran, can exert a tremendous influence. When everything is interconnected, a small player has the power to disrupt the system. Ironically it takes much more cooperation between dissimilar players to accomplish anything positive. The game is thus clearly asymmetrical. One tiny but negative force has the power to accomplish more.

Things do not happen for no reason. We lost the edge because however skillful managers and bureaucrats are at holding actions, they have no talent at all for advancing.

Thus America no longer leads the world, and is itself leaderless. The result, as on so many dimensions of our existence, is that unreality has become a substitute for what we lack.

The rebellion of the '60s, the Me Decade which followed, and today's yuppie society are all manifestations of the mistakes and crudities of the organization men. Many of our citizens have come to see America as the biggest, clumsiest, most mindless corporation of all, unable to find either its head or its heart. We are more divided than ever now: a nation of Me's.

But ignoring all the signals, along with their responsibilities, the managers and the bureaucrats continue to flex their considerable muscle. White House hired guns run illegal covert actions, while corporate hired guns gather their wagons in a circle, in preparation for the ultimate shoot-out. The virulent takeover fever now afflicting corporate America demonstrates not only the bankruptcy of its vision, but the desperation of the organization men as they try to consolidate and hold onto their power, or at least enrich themselves before they're run out of the game. For all their brass, these new business kingpins are not leaders, but merely bosses. If they continue unchecked, we may wake up one morning to find that all the major companies have taken over each other, and welded themselves into one mega-acronym—which does everything, but does nothing right, like the last dinosaur.

Like the dinosaur, these corporate takeover kings should be declared obsolete, for they mistake size or bigness for strength, confuse quantity with quality, and substitute ambition for imagination. Much like Washington's tin soldiers and sunshine patriots today, they do not understand the world as it has become. Indeed, they pander to its worst instincts by creating one of our hottest growth industries, i.e., the celebrity manufacturing industry.

In too many instances, horse and buggy minds are running the computers, minds that have been filled to the brim with trained incapacity. Our technological triumphs have outstripped our human accomplishments, and our miraculous machines make fools of us every day. America has been dragged, feet first, toward a new century. Or as we put it in Chapter Two, we are running 21st century systems of immense complexity with 19th century thinking.

Like the large old American car, the country seems to have gotten too big and too awkward to work very well, much less to respond quickly and wisely to events. Like its big corporations, the nation seems devoted to outmoded methods and ideas, and unwilling or unable to change direction, or even to recognize that it's foreign or domestic policies are not only outmoded, but dangerously insufficient.

As it turns out, the so-called breakthroughs of the 1960s were, in fact, breakdowns. We talked about freedom and democracy, but we practiced license and anarchy. People weren't as interested in new ideas as they were in recipes. Gurus Abraham Maslow and Carl Rogers told us we could create our own reality, and we did, but damned if we didn't just go for the gold again—like the 19th century robber barons. The primary lesson of the much-vaunted human potential movement was that we have far more potential for antisocial behavior than anyone had heretofore imagined. Thus it was that, in a less than sublime conjunction, the offspring of the allegedly radical movements of the 1960s found themselves in step with Ronald Reagan, the hero and spokesman for the far right, by 1980. With him, they believed that the individual was all, and greed was everything. Self interest was not only good, it was patriotic.

Historically, society ranked higher than the individual, and used him or her as it saw fit. Today, in America, the individual ranks higher than society, and uses it as he or she sees fit. There seems to be no such thing as the common good now, as everyone pledges allegiance to himself. What began as a kind of neopopulism has turned into plain old narcissism.

Freud said that each of us was three: id, ego and superego—more simply put, ambition, competence, and conscience or morality. In this age of narcissism, id is all. Our ambition, our greed has killed off conscience and morality, and made competency irrelevant. If competence counted for anything now, would rock singer Prince be king, and Sylvester Stallone, aka Rambo, get $16 million per extended grunt? Instead of leaders, we have celebrities and stars, specialists in solo turns, and we have McHeroes, like North, whom the media crank out in extraordinary numbers for our momentary delectation.

Alfred North Whitehead wrote, "In this modern world, the celibacy of the medieval learned class has been replaced by the celibacy of the intellect which is divorced from the concrete contemplation of the complete facts,"[3] and he didn't even know about the Wall Street insiders, the Iran/Contra scandal, or Gary Hart.

Ivan Boesky, Ollie North, and Gary Hart have, at least, celibacy of the intellect in common. They, like so many Americans now, are so egocentric, so absorbed in their own adventures that they see the rest of the world as an encumbrance, an annoyance. If the world had not got in their way, Boesky would still be running deals, North would still be running deals, and Hart would still be (is?) running for the presidency.

As Hart's farewell address so vividly demonstrated, he saw the flaw not in himself, but in us. Ollie North raged and wept at Congress's inability to understand that he was not only more patriotic, but braver and wiser than all of its members put together. Of course, this sort of intellectual celibacy is bound to turn into profligacy, and had Boesky, Hart or North engaged in the concrete contemplation of the complete facts, they might have saved themselves, and the rest of us, from their profligate actions. Hart, North and Boesky aren't exceptions, but the rule in a nation in which ambition has outstripped both competency and conscience.

Along these same lines, the captains of industry are back. It's almost impossible to pick up a book or watch TV or leaf through a magazine without getting one more report on America's superstar executives. Lee Iacocca, Ted Turner, Armand Hammer, T. Boone Pickens, Donald Trump, Victor Kiam, Sandy Sigoloff, Malcolm Forbes and Harold Geneen rank right up there with Stallone, Prince, Madonna, and the "Boss," Bruce Springsteen, because, to paraphrase the recent pop hit, we are a material people, ambition is good, and success is even better. In a nation full of people bent on acquiring status symbols, there is no higher status or more admirable symbol than the topmost rung on the corporate ladder. Once upon a time, we all wanted to be Charles Lindberg, or Joe DiMaggio, or Fred Astaire, because they were good, and now we want to be Pickens, Trump, or Iacocca, because they're rich.

But far too often these corporate stars, like their show biz and political counterparts, are empty suits, all sound and show signifying nothing. Of course, like their show biz and political counterparts, these corporate nabobs did not rise to the height unassisted. It has been our need as much as their greed which has catapulted them into the spotlight's golden glare.

At the heart of America is a vacuum into which self-appointed saviors and artificial creatures have rushed. They pretend to be leaders, and we—half out of envy and half out of longing—pretend to think of them as leaders. Consider that phenomenon, Ronald Reagan, the star who became a savior.[4] By 1980, Jimmy Carter had gotten us into a deep malaise. Then Ronnie rode in from the West, full of smiles and assurances, and he told us what we had been waiting to hear all our lives: that selfishness was OK.[5] In this way, the oldest President in history made us all feel young and strong again. America became a teenager, and so what if America ran amuck abroad and came unstuck at home? Ronnie kept smiling and kept us smiling.

Our need for true leaders goes unspoken, but manifests itself in pathetic ways—as in our idolatry of show biz stars, our admiration for corporate kings, and, most recently, our instant annointment of Ollie North. We don't much like what he did, according to pollsters, but we love the way that he did it.

Another manifestation of our need is the recent rash of instant leadership courses—which only goes to show how confused we are about what constitutes leadership. Some claim it derives wholly from power; others say it's nothing more than mechanics, a complete comprehension of the nature of organizations. Some say that leaders are born;

others argue that they can be made, and, according to the One Minute Manager or the Microwave Theory, made instantly. Pop in Mr. or Mrs. Average and out pops McLeader in sixty seconds. But billions of dollars are spent annually by and on would-be leaders, and we have no leaders, though many major corporations offer leadership courses to their more promising employees, corporate America has lost its lead in the world market. In fact, to this point, more leaders have been made by accident, circumstances, sheer grit or will than have been made by all the leadership courses. As Peter Drucker has noted, the most popular books which are sold annually are how to become a gourmet cook and how to lose weight. And yet, of course, these are the last things that can be attained from books alone. To that list must now be added how to become a true leader.

The Great Depression was the crucible in which Franklin D. Roosevelt was transformed from politician to leader. (In Joseph Campbell's terms[6] the Great Depression was the great event that signaled the beginning of FDR's long journey that ended with his attaining the status of a true hero.) Harry Truman became President when FDR died, but sheer grit made him a leader. Dwight Eisenhower seemed a likely winner to Republican Party bosses, but he stayed in office long enough to become his own man, and a leader to boot. Pols like Chicago's Mayor Richard Daley gave John Kennedy a boost into the White House, but he shone there on his own. Like them or not, FDR, Truman, Ike and JFK were all true leaders, in fact this nation's last true leaders. Truman never saw himself as a leader or made any effort to prepare for it. Eisenhower was a good soldier blessed with a constellation of better soldiers who ultimately made both his military and political victories possible. Those charming rich boys—Roosevelt and Kennedy—were, in the vernacular of the time, traitors to their class, but heroes to the people. To an extent, each of these men was his own invention: Truman and Eisenhower, the quintessential small town boys rising to the top; Roosevelt and Kennedy, driven by ambition and powerful parents, worldly, but conventional. Unlike today's instant heroes who are only bent on remaking themselves to fit in with the stereotypes of an existent public, they were bent on remaking both themselves and the world as well.

The true leader is not born, but made, and not made as much by others as by himself. But that of course is not all of it. Lyndon Johnson, Richard Nixon, and Jimmy Carter could reasonably be described as self-made men but they failed to win our hearts or engage our minds, and finally failed as leaders for several reasons.

All three were highly competent, but their ambitions overrode their talents. Johnson wanted to make a Great Society, but made a disastrous war instead. Nixon wanted less to lead us than to rule us, and it was never clear what Carter wanted, besides the White House. In each case, their minds seemed to be closed—to us, and perhaps even to themselves. Whatever vision each may have had went undeveloped and hence unexpressed. Each was given to saying one thing and doing another, and each seemed to look on the American people as adversaries. When we questioned the Vietnam War, Johnson questioned our loyalty. Nixon had an enemies list. And Carter accused us of malingering.

Johnson, Nixon, and Carter were all more driven than driving, and each seemed caught in his own shadows. They were haunted men, shaped far more by their early deprivations than by their later successes. They did not, then, invent let alone reinvent themselves, but were made, and then unmade by their own histories.

Just as Roosevelt and Kennedy made themselves new, and therefore independent and free, Johnson, Nixon, and Carter were used goods, no matter how far they got from their pinched beginnings or how high they rose.

It is no wonder that, in their wake, we took matters into our own hands. For as surely as Truman, Roosevelt, Eisenhower, and Kennedy invented themselves and Johnson, Nixon, and Carter were made by their own histories, we invented Ronald Reagan.[7] We made him a star, and then we made him President. It seemed perfect at the time—after all the good guys and all the bad guys, finally a *nice* guy made it to the White House. But it hasn't worked out very well.

The moment we decided we could make our own reality, what we have called unreality, we had no use for dreams. But as dreamless sleep is death, a dreamless society is meaningless. Since there is no such thing as a collective dreamer, we need dreamers—men and women who can express for and to us that irreverent, insouciant, peculiarly American spirit along with that passion for the promises of life which has been missing for so long. We need uncommon men and women who, having invented themselves, can now reinvent America.

Right now, there are probably several hundred thousand potential leaders in America—young passionate men and women full of promise with no outlets for their passion, because we scorn passion even as we reward ambition. If we can trust history, they're more likely to be the loners, the kids who always seem to be a little bit at odds with their peers, off there, looking at life from an odd angle. Leaders are always originals, not copies.

A leader, like anyone else, is the sum of all of his experiences, but, unlike others, he/she amounts to more than the sum, because he makes more of his experiences. Russ Ackoff once said that a system is never by definition merely the sum of its parts; it's either more or less. If it's merely the sum, then it's not a system for the parts have no bearing on one another. If it's less than the sum of its parts, then it's a system all right, but an ineffective one in that we have the case where the parts get in the way of one another. If it's more than the sum of its parts, then they're working together to bring out more between them. So it is we believe with leaders. They make positive use of their attributes to bring out more than is contained in their component parts alone.

This is the best and worst of all possible worlds for bright, young, would-be leaders: best because their opportunities for personal achievement are unlimited, worst because America has never been less interested in achievement or more interested in success. Everyone insists on having his own way now—from the President who sees Congress as his nemesis to the yuppie who shoves in at the head of the movie line. And yet it is precisely in those moments of greatest despair that thoughts that inspire originate. The words of Carl Jung come to mind: "Never is there more room for individuation in mass societies."

The contest between individual rights and the common good is far older than the nation, but has never been as fierce as it is today. In fact, as upwardly mobile man has replaced the average citizen, we have less and less in common and less and less that is good. The Founding Fathers based the Constitution on the assumption that there was such a thing as public virtue. James Madison wrote, "The public good...the real welfare of the great body of people...is the supreme object to be pursued...." At the moment, we not only can't agree what the public good is, we show little inclination to recognize it, let alone pursue it.

The notion of public virtue was replaced by special interests which was succeeded, in the 1960s, by values. Robert N. Bellah and his coauthors defined values in *Habits of the Heart*[8] as, "The incomprehensible, indefensible thing that the individual chooses when he or she has thrown off the last vestige of external influence and reached pure contentless freedom." The promise of the Great Society of the 1960s has been replaced by what Bellah, et al., called "a permissive therapeutic culture...which urges a strenuous effort to make our particular segment of life a small world of its own." People are literally retreating into their electronic castles, working at home and communicating with the world via computers, screening their calls on answering machines, ordering movies for the VCRs, food for their microwave ovens, and trainers for their bodies, and keeping the world at bay with advanced security systems. Trend spotters call this phenomenon "cocooning," but it might more accurately be described as terminal egocentricity.

As a nation can't survive without virtue, it can't progress without some common vision, and we haven't had a real sense of purpose, as a people, since the '60s. At no time in our history did the American people oppose government policies as vehemently as they did then. But instead of changing its policies, the government went underground, in the ultimate demonstration of cocooning.

Lyndon Johnson's lies about Vietnam, Nixon's Watergate, Jimmy Carter's disastrous dealings with the Shah of Iran, and Reagan's Iran/Contra double dealing all were part of an effort to deceive us, and Congress, not our enemies. When the outlaws are in the White House, both virtue and vision are absent by definition.

Too few leaders have, as we've said, a passion for the promises of life. Not surprisingly, young people have that very passion, until society extinguishes it. We must find the means not only to encourage that passion, but to nourish it—for our sakes as well as theirs.

A healthy, productive society is based on high expectations. The individual expects a society to be virtuous and just, while society expects him to be virtuous, productive, and committed. As the individual must continually challenge society to do better, society must, at the same time, ask much of its citizens. At the moment, neither the individual nor society seems interested in doing better—except on the most atavistic level. Society abuses us, and we use it. Nothing more, nothing less.

But since we are the society, we can't realistically expect *it* to do better until *we* do better, and we will not do better until we emerge from our cocoons and begin to engage the world. Vision, and virtue too, derive from such engagement, and from the full deployment of ourselves. Talent is one thing, as John Gardner has said, while its triumphant expression is another. Only when we are fully deployed are we capable of that triumphant expression.

The Greeks believed that excellence was based on a perfect balance of eros and logos, or feeling and thought, both of which derive from full engagement with the world on all levels. Our own narcissism coupled with the decline of universities from places of higher learning to high class vocational schools has made us not only selfish, but provincial as well.

But to become fully human one must know the world as well as oneself. Thornsten Veblen once said that Jews were so naturally intelligent because they were perpetual exiles. Exiles, wanderers, travelers not only see more, but see things fresh, because they have a different perspective.

Soviet leaders once called alleged troublemakers cosmopolitans, thereby complimenting them even as they
condemned them. Because they were essentially right;
troublemakers are cosmopolitan and cosmopolitans are
troublemakers. All the cliches about travel are true. It is a
great teacher. It does broaden. It clears our heads and
teaches us a thousand little things, and it is revelatory in
the extreme. It is impossible to spend two weeks in another
country without being altered in some way—unless, of
course, one is holed up in a club cocoon. Being on the road,
among strangers, not only requires the full deployment of
oneself, but redeploys oneself. Travel, or some sort of exile,
is as vital in the making of leaders as it is in that of the hero
himself. Roosevelt, Kennedy, and Eisenhower all traveled
extensively. Roosevelt, as a victim of polio, was often forced
to use a wheelchair, and that, in a way, was a form of exile.
Truman was in exile by virtue of his years of failure.
Johnson was a true provincial, never a citizen of the world,
always a citizen of rural Texas, which explains, at least in
part, why he failed as a world leader. Nixon and Carter did
actually travel, but they did not see anything, or learn,
being prisoners of their own provincial pasts.

The concrete contemplation of the complete facts means
idling, too. There, alone in a library, walking along an
empty beach or sitting at a sidewalk cafe, one has access to
one's soul.

But as much as one needs to wander alone—out in the
world and inside one's head—one needs mentors,[9] people
who offer both inspiration and example, who show us how
to be: a teacher who discovers gifts which one didn't know
were there, a writer who makes one see the world in an
entirely new way. Any good organization functions as a
kind of mentor, too, expecting more from its workers than
they knew they had to give, encouraging them to test
themselves and the organization, and experiment, which is
why perhaps there are so few truly good, let alone great,
organizations today. Today, organizations are more apt to
function like a 10K race. If you don't keep running and
running fast, you lose.

In the same way, most of our leaders also have benefited

from groups: the friends they grew up with, their wartime chums who got them through bad times. Sometimes, such groups simply sustain and encourage us, but sometimes they make history. The Bloomsbury writers...FDR's Brain Trust...Eisenhower's commanders...JFK's Irish Mafia...the Bauhaus designers...the painters and writers who gathered at Black Mountain College. G. Robert Oppenheimer directed what has been called the most exclusive club in the world at Los Alamos in the early years of World War II. He said of the scientists who had assembled to work on the atomic bomb, "It was a remarkable community inspired by a high sense of mission, of duty, and of destiny...coherent, dedicated, and remarkably selfless...devoted to a common purpose." In this age of ambition, community, common purpose, and the selfless dedication to the task at hand have become as passe as leaders themselves.

Education that is lifelong and drawn from many sources, travel, private lives, public association, mentors, all the pleasures and pains of real life, revelations, flubs are the raw ingredients of leadership. But even if one has all that, only he or she can put it all together and make it work, which is just as well, or we would end up with robots or, worse, beings from some artificial reality.

It is out of the broad, deep kind of life, this profound sort of experience and education that one develops taste, judgment, curiosity, energy and wit, along with virtue and passion.

Wit is the third rail of the intellect, enabling us to be simultaneously rational and intuitive, setting off that spark we usually call inspiration. Eros and Logos in perfect balance result in a healthy balance of faith and doubt, too—faith in oneself and abilities and in the world's possibilities, along with sufficient doubt to question, challenge, and probe, and thereby improve the world and oneself.

A leader doesn't just practice his profession or vocation, he masters it. He adapts, imagines, reverses, connects, compares, rejects, incubates, plays, and then he surrenders—in the way that an Arthur Rubinstein, having mastered the work, surrendered to it, became one with it, so that we could not tell where Rubinstein stopped and the music started. Roosevelt, Truman, Eisenhower, and Kennedy mastered the presidency. Johnson, Nixon, and Carter were mastered by it.

Such mastery requires absolute concentration or what the Japanese call *zanshin*. Rubinstein had it, so did Fred Astaire, and Martin Luther King; that's what got our attention before they actually said or did anything. King galvanized America with one speech. If we had read it, we might have seen it as rhetorical excess, but when King spoke, he didn't simply have a dream, he became the dream. He was the dream. That is *zanshin*, in full deployment of the self, and that, of course, is leadership in the truest sense of the term.

It is also a prime example of something we call resonance, a term we borrowed from the Canadian philosopher Northrop Frye. Resonance can't be taught or learned, and it is what separates true leaders from everyone else. To paraphrase Frye, resonance gives a particular person in a particular context universal significance. For a moment anyway, Martin Luther King's dream became our dream. He responded to some deep unspoken need in us, and imposed himself on our consciousness forever. Performers often have this sort of resonance. John Wayne, Marilyn Monroe, James Dean, Elvis—they answered some unspoken need in all of us, and we can still see them in our mind's eye, whole and intact. Certain objects, like the Statue of Liberty, also resonate in us, and certain times and places do as well; Athens and Israel, for instance, become a part of the collective map of our imaginative world. All these people, places, and things resonate with meaning far beyond their original context.

But resonance is a dicey quality. Chance Gardiner, the illiterate gardener in *Being There* who consumed and was consumed by television, became famous for such pseudo profundities as "In a garden, growth has its season. There are spring and summer. But there are also fall and winter. And then spring and summer again, as long as the roots are not severed, all is well and all will be well." No one knew what he was talking about, but everyone quoted him, including the U.S. President, because it all sounded good.

Ronald Reagan rode into office on pure resonance. No one had been more thoroughly initiated in the rituals of the all-American way than he, and no one was better suited to act out those rituals on the quintessential American medium, TV, than he.[10] He was the perfect embodiment of The Way. The ancient messages travel through him into the shining ether without friction. Ronald Reagan was the superconductor of our minds. It was as if his believing self was plugged directly into our wellsprings of belief, activating our desire to believe.

He did not argue for the American way, he *was* the American way. He didn't have to persuade us of anything. He merely had to appear. As was once said of Roy Larson of Time, Inc., he didn't have his finger on the pulse of America, he was the pulse. Reagan's approach was not didactic or discursive or sequential. It was associative, strobe-like, the all inclusive montage. We made the necessary connections. It wasn't his movie it was ours.

But resonance, like its first cousin luck, is fragile. It vanishes when its basis vanishes. We trusted Ronald Reagan, and now we don't. He became suddenly irrelevant, like the rich old uncle who turns up at family parties and tells long, pointless jokes. We laugh dutifully, but more at him than with him anymore. And we wish he'd just go home.

None of Reagan's would-be successors has anything like resonance. Like him now, they seem irrelevant. At the time of the initial writing of this book, the election was less than a year away, but we were already bored with the campaign. Democrats and Republicans alike study polls, instead of us, look at data, instead of the country, not realizing that we're so muddled we don't know what we want or even need. We saw Ollie North and thought we wanted him, but we're not so sure anymore. Anyway, he has already vanished. The dolls of his likeness are already thrown out with yesterday's towels.[11]

But we need dreamers now, and leaders, people of vision, virtue and passion who can lead us back to reality.

Which brings us to the gut question. Can leadership be taught, learned, somehow absorbed? Yes and no. Corporate colleges—such as Apple and AMI—and certain universities, recognizing the need for charismatic leadership, are attempting to teach such hitherto ignored disciplines as vision and virtue, along with communication and self-management skills. Fairly reliable data show that people can learn to be more creative, more visionary, and can develop more congruence between their own and society's concerns. But, at best, this is only behavior modification, and in any case, leadership is finally a collaborative endeavor.

As Lao Tzu said, to lead, one must follow. The leader must have virtue and vision, and some abiding passion, but he must also understand and be understood by his followers. Leadership is not some fixed capacity, but rather a talent for not just riding, but anticipating the next wave. It is messy, volatile and perilous work—which is why leaders sometimes get shot, and managers hardly ever do.

But true leadership goes even farther and deeper. It not only understands the unique source and form it takes in a particular individual, but it understands as well the broader dimensions of leadership. If all of us as a society are to move beyond our current preoccupation with unreality as substitutes for dealing with reality, then all of us must understand these dimensions as well.

A good friend and colleague, Will McWhinney, has invented a very powerful metaphor for helping us to see precisely these dimensions. McWhinney calls them the four levels of reality. They are most easily grasped in terms of four levels or different types of games.

Consider the game of chess. Level one is the competency to which we have referred earlier. It is the condition where one plays the game of chess as it is given to us or determined by others outside of our control. The best one can do at this level is to play as competently as possible *within the given rules of the game*. Competency thus becomes its own reward for play at this level, which is obviously not leadership. It is the level primarily by which technicians play.

Level two play is the ability to set the rules by which games at level one are played. The primary objective of level two is thus the securing of power. It's obvious that this level corresponds to what we have previously called ambition and, as we have said, it is a necessary condition of leadership. Obviously leaders must both be competent and possess ambition. No one denies this, but in themselves these two capabilities are not sufficient. In fact, if they are pursued almost exclusively, they lead as in the case of Johnson and Nixon to the loss of leadership.

Level three is where both players abandon challenging one another. They give up the notion of an "us" versus "them." They both agree to sit on the same side of the game board in order to play cooperatively, e.g., in the case of the U.S. and the Soviet Union, to set up joint cooperative defense systems. At this level, the realization occurs that in a world as compex and as interactive as today's, there is no such thing for any major power as security without joint mutual security. This level thus requires a deep ability to trust one's fellow players.

It is obvious that true leadership taps deeply into level three, which has always been the fundamental wellspring for dreams, for visions. Only at level three do we get to ethics, which is why Judge Robert Bork failed so miserably during his confirmation hearings for the Supreme Court. Bork was at best a player, like so many others in our society, at levels one and two. He could not grasp fundamentally that there was a sense of privacy and justice that went beyond strict rules and formulas which by definition can only be spelled out precisely at levels one and two. Indeed, level three moves beyond rules.

Level four is the most profound of all, for it moves beyond one of the few remaining limitations of the previous levels, the need for trust that fundamentally characterizes play at level three. At level four, the most profound question of all occurs, i.e., why are we playing games at all? Why are we not acting to better the human condition? Is this not precisely the question that has moved all truly great leaders?

At level four, one acts on what one personally envisions,

feeling deeply that it is somehow right for all mankind. A prominent example is Gandhi. One does what one feels is right whether one completely trusts one's adversaries or not. Of course, narrow and selfish feelings alone are not the criteria for action at this level, for if this were the case, then the crazy hallucinations of a Hitler would be equal to the visions of a Gandhi. The critical difference is that the leader at this level acts on his or her feelings by being in touch with the best instincts of all mankind, not the sickest impulses.

Is it not obvious that our preoccupation with unreality comes out of our failures as a society to nurture visions and dreams which can only arise from level four? Is it not equally obvious that the managers of the entertainment industry operate primarily at levels one and two at best and that in fact they have no interest whatsoever, assuming that they could even understand them to begin with, in moving to levels three and four? After all, what money is there to be made on levels three and four? The real paradox is that there is all the money in the universe to be made on these levels, but once one reaches them making money is no longer the chief goal.

There are many would-be heroes/leaders among us, and we have more means than ever before for helping them to realize their potential. But, for the moment, we don't want heroes/leaders. In these mean, greedy times, we prefer co-conspirators, and that is exactly what we have got—in the White House, the corporate boardrooms, and even in America's classrooms. There is, then, no doubt that we can do better and indeed must do better. But there is considerable doubt as to whether we want to, and so we are destined to drift on dreamlessly, secure in our cocoons of self interest.

8. The Metaphysics of Sappiness
The Primitivization of the American Intellect

...the "character issue"—a catch-all covering almost any action or utterance that seems to reveal a candidate's innermost self—has taken on a major role in the unfolding melodrama of President making, 1988 style.

The importance of the character issue, analysts say, reflects certain fundamental realities about the current struggle for the White House.

One is that there is not much else for candidates and voters to focus on. Major ideological differences within each party are absent; the candidates are in general agreement about ends, and their haggling over means is not particularly dramatic.

Nor is there an overriding issue, such as war or depression, to command the voters' attention. *It's not that the nation lacks problems but that the problems are so complex and interrelated that it is next to impossible for candidates to propose solutions that are both appealing and credible* [italics ours].

"In the great depression, great ideas were generated," said Columbia University historian Henry Graff, a specialist in the Presidency. But given the confliting global and domestic pressures of the 1980s, he said, "problems come at you from left and right, and the public knows there is no quick answer."[1]

"Nancy Reagan invited Alf to the White House last week to entertain at a children's Christmas party. There, Alf discovered that the President, the First Lady and his daughter Maureen are three of the millions of adult fans nationwide who have rocketed what many critics initially dismissed last season as a silly children's show into the Nielsen Top 15.

"If Alf ran for President—and he's a lot like Mario Cuomo at this point," says Tom Pachett, executive producer and co-creator…, "I'll bet he would get over three million votes."

Alf's own sense of humor is really quite juvenile. He burps, dresses up in women's jewelry and laughs at his own inane jokes. But he is also outspoken, uninhibited and unencumbered by normal human rules of etiquette and conversation. The adorable alien exposes the foibles and absurdities of suburban living, and it's his fundamental honesty and the simple outrageousness of Alf's adopted family—four otherwise sane and exceedingly normal human beings—actually carrying on regular human conversations with him, Patchett says, that has charmed the adult audience as well as the children.

"He says what we are all thinking in the back of our minds but are always afraid to say out loud," says Paul Fusco, the show's producer and the man who created Alf.

"So many people want to believe he's real," Fusco says. "Alf is in fact very real to me. He has his own dressing room. He speaks for himself. I prefer to preserve that. When you know how it's done, it's not just as fascinating anymore."[2]

All theses, even the best supported, face difficulties. The world is just too complex to be explained by any single thesis no matter how plausible it is. And when the thesis advanced is controversial to begin with—especially when for ease of discussion it is presented without the large number of qualifiers that inevitably accompany any bold proposal—then it is guaranteed to provoke a raft of objections. One should not therefore be surprised to find that on those occasions when we have presented the thesis publicly, the general thesis of unreality provokes strong reactions. Indeed, when they have been critical, there are two general types or categories of reactions to the general notion of unreality as we have developed it:

— qualitative,
— quantitative.

The qualitative reactions question fundamentally whether we have gotten the basic phenomenon of unreality right to begin with. The quantitative reactions question whether we have overexaggerated its degree of importance. Some typical qualitative criticisms are as follows:

— What's new? It's always been the same.
— News has always been entertaining.
— Aren't we really assuming what we have only pretended to deny, i.e., that there "really is" an untarnished reality "out there" unaffected by human minds?
— Aren't we just old fashioned moralists reacting like old fashioned moralists always have, i.e., resisting, not to say misunderstanding seriously, the structure of the new electronic world that is emerging? Wouldn't we be better off describing and analyzing objectively and impersonally what this new order is instead of judging it from the standards of the past?

Some typical quantitative concerns are:

— Are conditions really any worse today?
— Aren't we naively assuming that there was a time, some Golden Past, when mankind was somehow free of unreality? If anything, the case can be made that the excesses of the past far exceeded ours.

There are no fully adequate, let alone completely convincing, responses to these criticisms for the same reason that there are no fully airtight demonstrations of their truth. Nevertheless, they deserve a response if only for the reason that the objections are worthwhile in themselves. Thus, our responses to them help to clarify our position further even if they run the risk of appearing defensive.

We are the first to admit that we are not professionally trained historians. This does not mean that we ridicule or devalue history as an important discipline as so many academics devalue fields outside of their own narrow expertise. We are only admitting our ignorance, not a fundamental lack of appreciation for the importance of history as a discipline. Indeed, history is one of human-kind's most important fields of study. Without the concept of history, the concept of "humankind" is itself lame. Without history, we are not able to know intelligently the range of possible behaviors that characterize us as a species, what, in short, is the general measure of human-kind. Thus, were not able to judge whether the unreality of our age differs significantly in intensity or degree (i.e., quantitatively) from that of previous eras. But to a signifi-cant extent, the determination of intensity is not absolutely critical to our major thesis.

A major part of our effort has been Kantian in spirit. We have been motivated to show how unreality, to use Kant's phrasing, is "possible." That is, what are the mechanisms by which it is possible to manufacture unreality? From this standpoint, the question whether earlier ages were more or less "unreal" than ours is beside the point. It is akin to asking Kant whether the conditions he specified that were necessary for the possibility of human knowledge were more or less "true" in earlier eras. The question is to a large extent meaningless. One either possesses the mecha-nisms that are necessary to know reality or one does not. By the same token, one either has identified the mecha-nisms necessary for the production of unreality or one has not. Whether earlier ages made more or less use of these or other mechanisms is another question, one that is no less important, but still another question.

The Kantian parallel with unreality is of course neither perfect nor exact. One can contend legitimately that the mechanisms for the production of unreality are culturally and historically bound, and this we do not deny. One can also contend legitimately that the mechanisms have changed over the course of history. And this we not only deny but indeed affirm. But as we have said earlier, our major purpose has not been primarily historical. We have not endeavored to show the historical evolution of unreality but rather to show the mechanisms responsible for its production in our time and the prominent place that unreality occupies in our culture.

Of course, ultimately our thesis, like all theses, depends on a comparative assessment as to whether unreality has been more or less abundant than in previous eras. However, even without this full assessment, we can be confident that we have continually evolved the kinds of unreality and the mechanisms for their production. Indeed, one of our primary contentions is that unreality is always dependent upon the technology available at the time. From this standpoint, we have a reason to believe that unreality, like all things human, changes in response to human needs.

In this regard, we certainly have not assumed that the U.S. is first among the so-called civilized or developed nations in its production and use of unreality. If we have made it appear at times that among the developed societies of the world the U.S. is most advanced in its production and use of unreality, then this is only because we are closest to U.S. culture. Thus, to a certain extent we can see our own unreality better than we can see that of others. However, the more one studies other cultures, the more one finds unreality's universal appeal:

> The ordinary-ordinary and the famous-ordinary interact directly in the many audience-participation programmes on Japanese television. At peak viewing times about one-third of the output is devoted to quiz, game and amateur talent shows, many of them of a vulgarity unparalleled anywhere in the world. In *The Endurance*, groups of students compete in the performance of such tasks as crawling through tubes filled with snakes and lizards. In the various *Love Clinic* programs, newly-wed couples are interrogated by smarmy comedians on the details of their sex life. For both viewers and participants the attraction lies not in the prizes on offer, indeed there are often no prizes at all. The

point is in the participation itself, the intimate relation between the watchers and the watched. In *Cheerful TV* dozens of ordinary people—doctors, bus drivers and secretaries—crowd around with Japan's most famous "talents," performing elaborate mass charades in the streets of Tokyo.

The Japanese inhabit a scaled-down version of McLuhan's global village, their sense of group values being reinforced by the vast quantity of vicarious experience they have consumed together, more powerful than anything the individual encounters in his everyday life. Small wonder that cable TV has never caught on: what is being sought is not choice but mass intimacy. The cathode ray spirits which visit Japanese homes every night have assumed the function that the prewar symbol of national identity has vacated. The programs themselves may not be much good as entertainment, but they have succeeded in meeting social needs far more profound.[3]

Even if the unreality of our times were no greater than that of previous eras, this in itself would be no cause for rejoicing or lack of concern. Because humans have always engaged in undesirable activities such as child abuse or family violence, this is no excuse for our acceptance of them. As we know all too well, the "socially accepted problems" or "unchangeables of the human condition" of one era, e.g., racial prejudice, slavery, have become the great social causes of another. Rather than being permanent unchanging features of the human condition, in some cases, such as slavery, they have been greatly eradicated.

Above all, the one thing we have not assumed is that reality, especially its knowledge by humans, is independent of our minds, needs, and social purposes. The very description of reality is shot through and through with human needs, passions, emotions. It is also strongly affected by the nature of our minds and the general culture of which we are a part. For instance, human language plays such a strong and vital role in the description of, not to say the basic human ability to experience, reality, that it is impossible to sever completely the connection between what is known from the nature of the knower.

Consider, for instance, the literally earth-destroying "fact" of nuclear weapons. The very term "weapons" itself connotes a social reality—that nuclear weapons are like any others in that they can actually be used against an enemy. And yet, the world is inescapably coming to the conclusion that the term "nuclear weapons" is an oxymoron. Nuclear "devices" are not "weapons" in the classical sense of the term for they can *not* be used against an enemy without causing severe if not just as much damage to the attacker as to the attacked. Since they cannot be uninvented scientifically, they must be reinvented socially, i.e., placed in another social category which in effect prescribes their "new reality" by limiting their use.

This has been one of our major points all along. One does not require the existence of some Golden Past—a world free from unreality—to be concerned about unreality in the present and especially in the future. Indeed, we are not worried about some Golden Past as much as we are concerned about some Golden Future that our technology is supposed to create.

We should make clear another point. We are not opposed to technology per se. Indeed, one of us (Mitroff) has a Ph.D. in Engineering from one of this country's leading engineering schools (University of California at Berkeley) while the other (Bennis) has one of the first Ph.D.'s in economics that was granted from one of the world's leading technological institutes (MIT). Thus, we are not opposed in principle to the existence of a media lab at MIT which in our view is devoted to the production of devices that will alter significantly how we experience as well as interact with our environment. We believe that it is fundamentally in the province of humankind to shape and reshape its world. Humankind does not merely experience reality but fundamentally creates it. Experimentation with reality is thus a deep part of our nature.

What we are adamantly opposed to is the separation of ethics and social forecasting from the day to day development of technology. As we noted in Chapter Two, the separation of the forecasting of the social consequences of technologies from those could only work in a world that had very long lead times between the invention of a technology and its widespread adoption, and therefore more exact knowledge of its consequences, both good and bad. Again, as we argued in Chapter Two, we no longer have the buffer or slack available in our civilization to adopt a wait and see attitude. By definition, if a "system" is any one thing, it is *not* separable into its various aspects. Thus, we are not, we hope, "old fashioned moralists" as much as we are "new fashioned systems thinkers" for whom explicit ethical judgments are integral parts of the systems approach.[4]

We openly admit that we are polemicists in that we do not believe that one can describe "objectively" any important social phenomenon independently of making strong judgments about it. For this reason alone, readers deserve to see our judgments whether they necessarily agree with them or not, and, in fact, all the better that they do not, so they can form their own judgments and reach their own conclusions. We reject vehemently the notion that one can be neutral on important or social matters. We might in fact agree more with those who have criticized our stance were they not equally vehement in their adoption of a stance of "neutrality."

With these thoughts in mind, let us then turn to a recapitulation of the thesis of this book and an assessment of what if anything can be done about what we take to be a "real" problem and one that will only get "more real" as time unfolds.

The Gigantic Morality Play That Is Contemporary America

The central thrust of this book has been that America today can only be understood in terms of a gigantic morality play. As important as it is, more than America's economic future alone will be determined by the forces involved in shaping this play. The forces involved will also test and determine the fate of America's very character and soul—insofar as whatever still remain of them are left to be determined.

Two general sets of forces operate that will determine America's short-term and long-term destiny. The first set, which formed the basis of our discussions in Chapters Two and Seven, emanates from the new global reality. This part of America's morality play we call the "Complexity From Without."

The second set comes from the tremendous power and influence that the general TV, show-business, entertainment and celebrity-manufacturing culture wield on every facet of our society. This part of America's morality play which we discussed in Chapter Three onward we call the "Rot From Within."

The Complexity From Without describes the new highly interdependent, highly coupled global economy and world that have arisen since World War II, but more especially in the last five to ten years. The net effect of the global economy is that *everything* is not only interconnected but potentially capable of affecting everything else. As we have emphasized, the result is that everything everywhere has now become local news. In case there be any doubt, one need only mention again Bhopal and Chernobyl. The world is a far more complex and chaotic place than anything our ancestors ever envisioned or had to face. As a consequence, the rules of doing business have changed so radically that entirely new ways of thinking are needed if all businesses, let alone nations as a whole, are to survive in today's environment.[5]

To put this part of the play or drama in psychoanalytic terms, the human ability to handle the Complexity From Without calls for the most mature ego and superego. It also calls for the ability to leave aside and go beyond old habits, fixed stereotypes, ideologies, and ingrained prejudices so that one can get on with the fundamental job of dealing with new realities, which by definition are the quintessential tasks of a mature ego and superego. Thus, the protagonists on one side of America's morality play are the forces—*if any*—promoting the development of America's ability to deal honestly, comprehensively, and systematically with the realities of the new economy.

To face reality, for instance, Americans will have to

acknowledge forthrightly that we now have a second-rate educational system no longer capable of producing, for the most part, workers who have the necessary understanding of complex technology in order to produce quality goods that can compete in a global economy. Compared to the Japanese, the statistics are truly frightening.[6] The illiteracy rate in Japan is less than one percent, and this for one of the world's most difficult languages to learn. Depending upon how one measures it, our national illiteracy rate is 20 percent and higher. The Japanese "mathematical" literacy rate is even more astounding. In a comparison of scores of high school seniors, Japan's youth came in first out of ten industrialized nations; the U.S. last. Only the African and Third World countries were behind the U.S. We pay lip service to excellence—we hype it like everything else we do—but until we take excellence seriously we're bound to be a nation of mediocrities.

Crowding, if not crashing, up against the Complexity From Without is the Rot From Within. This part of America's morality play has to do with the general effects of the larger TV and show business culture, of which increasingly every facet of our society from education to politics is affected, on our growing *inability* to handle complex issues.

The argument has been essentially this: By the very nature of the medium, TV works by breaking everything down into 15-to-30 second segments or blips. Since the primary purpose of each blip is to grab and to hold the attention of the viewer, the content of any blip is nowhere as important as who delivers it and how the presenter looks. The primary purpose of TV is not to inform or to educate, and even strangely enough not to entertain, but to keep the viewer from switching dials by holding his or her attention. But to do this requires a never ending series of quick, almost totally unrelated, attention grabbers. Nothing more, nothing less is the intention. The result for an increasingly complex society in an interdependent world can be devastating.

When TV becomes the primary source of "news-enter-tainment" (or "newstaint," to coin a word), and when no 15-

to 30-second blip need bear any logical or coherent relationship to any other blip, and when blips follow one another faster than anyone can make sense of them, the inevitable result not only is a society that is uninformed about anything, but one that has lost the even more fundamental ability to know that it is uninformed. In short, *it is ignorant of the fact that it is ignorant. It doesn't know that it doesn't know.* Worse yet, it may have lost the ability and the very soul to care. For without the basic intellectual faculty to relate what is said in one 15- to 30-second segment to what is said in another, one has lost the critical ability to make sense of a thought pattern (for example, the statement of any complex problem) that takes longer than 15- to 30-seconds to utter and hence to process.

In psychoanalytic terms, the counter-protagonist, as represented by TV and show business, to that of the mature ego and superego demanded by the new global economy is an incredibly primitive intellect—in other words, Freud's id. In effect, as the new global economy requires a greater or more mature intellect on the part of the general populace of Western democracies, the increased power of the media has contributed to the greater primitization of the intellect.

We must appreciate that both phenomena, the Complexity From Without and the Rot From Within, are fundamental aspects of the Systems Age. It is highly tempting to argue that the reasoning or general processes of thinking that we believe are necessary to cope with the Complexity From Without are characteristic of earlier eras, what some communication theorists such as Meyrowitz[7] have called the Age of Print. Likewise, it is further tempting to argue that what we have called the Rot From Within is characteristic of the Electronic Age of which TV may be the archetypal representative.

According to this argument, conventional reasoning, rationality in general, is characteristic to a print culture, which is ordered hierarchically in its progression of thought. Thus, in the Age of Print, books are ordered both in their degrees and levels of difficulty. One progresses, as it were, from elementary books on a subject in grammar school to advanced texts in the university. In short, in the Print Age, learning demands that one has met certain prior prerequisites before moving on.

In contrast, TV, as the prime representative of the Electronic Age, imposes little if any prerequisites on the viewer. One can watch anything irrespective of age, sex, social class, religion, etc. From this perspective, there is no such thing as "children's TV," since all of TV is more widely accessible to the eyes of children than we would like to believe. To be sure, what one "sees" is dependent upon one's level of education, maturity, social class, and so forth, but the basic point is that one can watch just about any program without having had to progress through formalized TV instruction.

While these observations are correct in general, we believe they miss a fundamental point. *Both* the Complexity From Without and the Rot From Within are characteristic of the Systems Age, and in this sense, of the Electronic Age.

The Electronic or Systems Age calls for *more, i.e., greater, understanding,* not less, but of a fundamentally different kind from that which characterized the Machine Age. All eras and phenomena which are complex are characterized by parallel phenomena or cross-currents that occur simultaneously. Thus, the Systems Age calls for a greater rationality but of a different kind in order to cope with all the complexity it raises up in greater abundance. In other words, the Systems Age produces simultaneous forces which demand greater competency while strangely enough at the same time promote greater incompetency. It is therefore not the case that competency or rationality alone belongs to an earlier era and incompetency or noncompetency belongs to ours, but rather that both are deep characteristic features contemporarily.

It is also vitally important to appreciate that the properties of TV as a medium neither exist nor operate in isolation by themselves. TV is embedded within the larger context of a vast multi-billion-dollar-a-year entertainment business. One of the most important and growing aspects of this larger entertainment business is the celebrity-manufacturing portion of it. When so much is at stake in terms of huge profits and when by the very nature of the medium it consumes "personalities" faster than they can be produced by natural means, then personalities have to be manufactured—created or invented—on demand according to pre-set specifications or formulas. Essentially the process is no different from manufacturing anything. Only the inputs and the outputs differ. In this case, the inputs are miniature "persons" blinded by the lure of big bucks, fame, ego gratification, etc., who offer themselves up "willingly" to be molded into celebrities, the outputs of the process. Depending upon the extent and the depth of the process involved, the final finished product *is* for all practical purposes a "new person." If the transformation process is "successful," little or nothing of the former or original self (product) will remain. The end products will have internalized the new role so deeply that they will have become virtually identical with it.

Brilliant analysts of the media from Marshall McLuhan to Neil Postman, as well as a host of others, have looked at the epistemological properties of TV as a medium largely in a vacuum. (Classically, epistemology is that branch of philosophy which deals with such issues as: how do we know, what is valid knowledge, how do we know when we have it, and what can we know, i.e., what is knowable? The "epistemological properties of TV" refer to the kind of knowledge that is possible to gain from TV because of the type of medium that it is. Thus, as we have emphasized repeatedly throughout this book, TV knowledge is essentially visual, incoherent, frenetic, lacking context, without a larger framework to ground the images that are thrown at the viewer, and contradictory; i.e., essentially it is patternless knowledge, if that can be called knowledge at all in the classic sense of the term.)

For example, Neil Postman's most recent analysis[8] of TV remains essentially correct, *if* one looks only at the epistemological, i.e., surface, properties of TV as a medium primarily suited to expressing images, not ideas. That is, if one accepts the boundaries that Postman and others have placed implicitly on the examination of TV as a system, then one must reach essentially the same conclusions that they have: that TV is largely Huxleyian in both its hidden intent as well as explicit mode of operation. In other words, TV is not Orwellian in the sense envisioned by Orwell, nor does it employ overt "thought police" to control a population. The U.S. government controls neither the content nor the format of TV in the same way that totalitarian governments do. Further, neither the networks nor the state nor TV itself force the people to watch the tube. Rather, TV operates much more insidiously, lulling us silently and seductively into collective dumbness through its very banality.

It was Huxley's and secondarily Postman's brilliance to see the true danger behind TV's surface idiocy. The true danger they foresaw was that Western democracies would not be overtaken by what Robert Reich[9] has called the Mob At The Gates, or what others have called, The Evil Enemy, Empire, or Threat From Without. Rather, they foresaw that a much greater threat, precisely because it would not be viewed as a threat as such, was that the so-called "advanced" Western societies would be undermined by their own self-inflicted, endless pursuit of mindless pleasures and trivialities, e.g., drugs, TV, the endless consumption of junk food, useless material items, and trivializing ideas.

What McLuhan, Postman, and others have overlooked is that when one views TV as a medium *both* from within and from without at the same time, then a very different picture emerges. Internally, the Huxleyian properties of TV are still there. However, even internally, there are Orwellian properties of the medium of a very peculiar kind that have not been previously identified as such. In addition, when one looks at TV through the lens of the business of manufacturing celebrities, then what emerges are Orwellian aspects of TV beyond any reasonable doubt. The producing, selling, and consuming of celebrities include the full range of Orwellian techniques such as brainwashing, the use of double think, double talk, personality reshaping, etc.

The point of all this is that the tools and techniques used

to shape the personalities of celebrities constitute a political and a social "technology" in the broadest possible sense of the term. In the end, this technology shapes us as a culture as well. For in the act of manufacturing those few, revered others who exist to satisfy our deepest needs, we are engaged in the manufacturing and remanufacturing of ourselves as well.

Neil Postman has noted with insight that Americans today may be the best entertained but least informed people on the planet. He has also felt, as we have remarked on earlier, that when Americans meet it is no longer to discuss ideas or to share intellectual propositions, but rather to entertain one another. While these observations are "true" within Postman's framework, we think the situation has taken a dangerous, more ominous turn. Increasingly, Americans meet not only to entertain one another but to make and remake, to manufacture and remanufacture, themselves.

The "technologies" for producing celebrities have literally invaded and transformed the body politic, body social, and body moral of this society to such a degree that the understanding of how these technologies function and how they affect America's ability to function in a world of perverse complexity is a topic of the highest importance. How we came as a nation to the manufacturing of unreality on so large a scale and what this phenomenon portends for our future has been the subject of this book.

Because he had the extreme benefit of hindsight, the late Marshall McLuhan was able to analyze brilliantly the effect that the invention of the book in terms of Gutenberg's printing press had on the structure of the Western mind.[10] McLuhan made the case convincingly that the introduction of the book helped pave the way for Western, analytic thinking. Whereas before Gutenberg, men conversed in groups and exchanged communal stories, i.e., knowledge was transmitted and constituted orally, now they were isolated by the very nature of the new medium they had invented; they became isolated, solitary, individual readers. Further, because the medium of written language required a clear exposition of a "this" before a "that," it needed a linearity of thinking that in effect was the precursor of the industrial revolution. The book contributed to the perception and organization of the world into fragmented parts. In other words, the book contributed to the breakup of the world into separate units.

When one is living as we are through a revolution as profound as any that has occurred in human affairs, we don't have the luxury of hindsight. All we can do is study ourselves during the process of reinventing ourselves. One thing, however, seems clear. If Gutenberg's printing press helped pave the way for the industrial revolution and the mechanical view of the universe and even of man that it unleashed, then the latest modes of expressing ourselves are helping to pave the way for the next stage of man. What choice is there then but to understand them if we are to understand ourselves? Unless, that is, we are by now so much under the influence of the newer media that "understanding" as we have known it, i.e., as a capacity to be engaged in and developed by educated and civilized people, almost for its own sake, is a queer item from the past.

The central issues are no longer that the vast majority of commercial TV is irredeemable junk and that celebrity worship has reached such vast proportions and has infiltrated our society to such a degree that it constitutes an unhealthy sore on the body politic. However debatable the truth and the merit of these propositions (for contentiousness is part of the core makeup of all basic issues), we take it nonetheless that they have been sufficiently well established by others that we have regarded them as provisional working hypotheses or jumping off points for our examination.

Our concerns lie much deeper. We are concerned with the soul of present day America. We are concerned with how our nation can compete economically against other nations such as Japan which still regard education as the fundamental infrastructure of their society.[11] What, in short, can be the fate of a society such as ours where the body politic has been so invaded by a cult of celebrity that the manufacturing of celebrities is in many senses our fundamental business and infrastructure?

Our concern is, therefore, with the rules of knowing and of valuing which underlie the media and the celebrity manufacturing industry. How do the kinds of knowledge and values that these industries promulgate affect our society? These have been our questions.

In a recent book that deserves to be read,[12] *The Last Intellectuals* (not because like all polemics it is entirely correct, but because it helps us to see a serious issue that we need to face), Russell Jacoby has bemoaned the fact that we Americans seem to have lost one of our great traditions. We are no longer producing a new generation of public intellectuals. In their place, perhaps because of the vacuum that has been created by their absence, we have developed a fondness for what we can only label the metaphysics of sappiness. This metaphysics is manifested by a culture that gives prominence to hack writers and third-rate thinkers. These are the role models to which as a society we increasingly turn for illumination on the issues of our day or perhaps more accurately to avoid illumination on the issues of our day. We quote:

> ...[Danielle Steel] is real enough to her adoring public to have been named one of the ten most influential women in the world in a 1981 national poll of college students. To have a million copies of her newest novel printed in hardcover, with an additional four million slated for paperback. To have eighty-five million copies of her books in print worldwide.
>
> [To quote from Steel herself:] "When it's 1:30 or 2:00 in the morning and I feel like reading something, I don't want to read Thomas Mann. I want to read Jackie Collins. Some long esoteric treatise may be good for your mind, but it's awful hard to read. And after you pass the age of twelve, you have enough pressure and stress that you just want something you can flow with."[13]

> "So," I [Shirley MacLaine] said anxiously, in finding myself slightly breathless, "so I lived way back in some ancient civilization?"
>
> "Yes, several times," said John. "Twice as a male and once as a female."
>
> I was quiet as one of the finer points of reincarnation hit

home again. "Have we all experienced living as different
sexes in order to be able to empathize with the opposite
sex?"

"That is correct," said John. "Certainly. How else could
mankind reach such an understanding of itself and its
identities without such diversified physical experiences?"

I leaned forward again. "Could that be a metaphysical
explanation for homosexuality?" I asked. "I mean, maybe a
soul makes a rocky transition from a female to a male body,
for instance, and there is left over emotional residue and
attraction from the previous incarnation?"

...Jesus, I thought, maybe time and space are so relative
they are not measurable. Maybe they both exist at the same
time. Maybe the soul inside my body was telling me that
everything is real. And if that was true, then reality had more
dimensions than I had ever considered. Perhaps, as philoso-
phers and even some scientists claim, reality was only what
one perceived it to be.

If that were the case, I could understand on a colossal
scale what an added spiritual dimension could mean to the
planet and the human beings living on it. What a wonder,
what a marvel that would be!

Everyone's perception of reality would be valid. If the
soul's experience was all that mattered and one's physical
existence was literally irrelevant because, from a cosmic
perspective, there was no such thing as death, then every
living second on earth was precious precisely because it *did*
relate to a grand overall design *which we had helped to create*,
and precisely because every *atom* had a purpose, maybe the
purpose of this particular collection of atoms writhing
around here on the bed was to convey the message that we
are a part of the God-force that created all things....[14]

In the end we must confront the question, "What in
God's name have we become?" What can we hope for the
fate of our children when so much now depends on how we
face honestly and grapple with all the forces that have been
leashed by the Complexity From Without?

What Is to Be Done?

Much as we would desire it, our purpose in writing this
book has not been to offer a detailed solution to a problem

as complex as the one we have been addressing. Our main concern has been one of stating the problem itself correctly in the first place, of offering a broad framework that recognizes as many of the problem's dimensions as possible so that if a solution is possible in the future, it can be produced.

A problem as complex as the one we have been exploring throughout this book of necessity calls for a number of responses from a multitude of parties across many different levels and layers of our society. If we learn one thing and one thing only about complex systems, it should be this: systems of vast complexity cannot be controlled by mechanisms that are at a level of complexity less than the system which they are attempting to control. If the control mechanism is less complex than that of the system it is attempting to control, then the control will make the original system worse off. As we noted in Chapter Two, no better example exists than the recent crash of the stock market. The human and technical systems were not able to cope with the complexity of the very system they had helped create.

A number of responses to the problem of unreality we have been exploring can be discussed.

At the end of his book, *Amusing Ourselves to Death*, Neil Postman eschews virtually any use of TV, e.g., his appearing on TV in order to make use of the very medium of which he is so highly critical in order to reform it. We don't necessarily share Postman's feelings, for as we have indicated we don't believe that the properties of "the medium" are solely contained within it.[15] As we have attempted to make clear, the properties of TV are the result of a very complex interaction among the technical characteristics of the medium itself, the psychological properties of viewers, the structural properties of the entertainment industry, and the properties of the larger American culture within which all of the above are embedded. Public TV certainly shows that it need not be a medium that is primarily geared to our basest archetypal tendencies as well as hyperactive needs. Indeed, programs such as *Masterpiece Theater* and *Wonderworks* demonstrate that characters as fine, as complex, and as subtle as any that are drawn from the great novels can be presented in a manner that does admirable justice to them. To do so, however, *Masterpiece Theater* and *Wonderworks* have to go directly against the grain of American culture. They have to induce a deep process of getting to know the characters where "knowing" is based on slowing down, of listening attentively to good conversation, words, phrases, and ideas that elevate and show the best that humans can attain. All these characteristics of course are probably anathema to a mass audience, but they are limitations of the audience not fundamental characteristics of the medium. After all, shoddy goods are merely characteristic of shoddy producers, not necessarily fundamental attributes of the products themselves. In the same regard, it should also be mentioned that commercial TV likewise is capable on occasion of providing excellent shows on serious topics for a mass audience. For instance, commercial TV has tackled with great sensitivity such topics as child abuse, battered wives, and AIDS when it has found commercial sponsors willing to support them.

For these reasons, we believe that a TV program on unreality is both necessary and desirable. Not to show the mechanisms that are involved in producing unreality when a fundamental aspect of their essense is visual, is literally to miss "seeing" them. A serious documentary on the abuses themselves does not have to condone or commit them. We are less willing to judge before such a program is produced what its effects would be. We refuse to believe that a society with as much creativity as ours cannot turn that same creativity to any topic it wishes to exercise it on.

To underwrite or produce such a program, or series of programs, however, will call for cooperation among diverse segments of our society. For one thing, the large foundations will have to come to see that the problem we and others have been addressing is as profoundly a serious threat to the health of the republic as are others. They will have to see that problems such as Boundary Warping and Image Engineering, to mention merely two, are as serious infectious diseases that threaten the health of our society as are biological diseases. They will have to understand this if they are to throw their potentially enormous support to such a project.

In the same vein, many more studies of the kind we have attempted here will have to be conducted. Of necessity, when a topic is so huge, so broad, and so relatively new, we could only hit its most prominent spots. Yet, the present topic is certainly deserving of much more systematic and interdisciplinary study precisely because it arises from the newly and increased interconnectedness of the world. To our knowledge, this is one of the very few studies that has even recognized the dual nature of the problem, i.e., that there is a *possible* relationship between what we have called the Complexity From Without and the Rot From Within. This is also one of the few studies that has attempted a systematic juxtaposition of the properties of both realms.

Many more studies are needed, however. For instance, it is still highly contested by political scientists[16] whether and how much TV actually influences public opinion on key issues and voting by the masses on critical races. Even by those who doubt the influence of TV on such matters, the measurements of public opinion are acknowledged to be highly sensitive on the ways in which questionnaires are presented to respondents. Thus, to our knowledge and satisfaction, we cannot gauge at this time the extent to which Boundary Warping, for instance, influences the general attitudes and opinions of the populace because we have not designed the proper instruments to measure the phenomenon. *How does one ask questions of that which one has not yet seen as a potential problem?*

Speaking of a populace leads to another posture towards the problem. Richard Schickel, for one, is extremely pessimistic about the ability of the masses to show any appreciation and concern for the problem we have been discussing. (So we might add are the authors of *High Visibility*, but they are obviously pessimistic for other reasons.) We must admit that we find Schickel's position extremely enticing. It is very easy to become pessimistic about any and all attempts to raise the general level of sophistication and awareness of a mass audience especially when there are so many forces arrayed against such an effort. The profits to be made in keeping the general level of mass appreciation low are enormous and getting bigger all the time.

And yet one must try lest one give up altogether. The attempts may well prove to be futile but what else is there for humans to do if they would keep alive some vestige of the hero archetype that resides in us all?

There are two more avenues we wish to touch on. There is no doubt that the FCC must play a major role, without imposing severe restrictions on freedom of speech and creativity. Studies must be commissioned which investigate feasible limits on the use of entertainment techniques and the development and presentation of news. No one wants to curtail freedom of speech or limit creativity, but careful thought needs to be given to those techniques and technologies that are deemed injurious and must be limited or controlled in some way. Undoubtedly new rules on the presentation of news will have to be developed.

One of the most important and troublesome cases is clearly that of TV news. Knowledge plays such an important role in modern societies that we are perhaps most deeply troubled of all by whether news can be reformed to give a mass audience the knowledge it now needs to function in a complex world. Given the current structure of TV news and the news organizations themselves, there may be no viable solution at the present time.

This in turn only raises further thorny issues that to our knowledge have not been addressed. The deepest are: what are the functions and forms of entertainment that are appropriate for the Systems Age? What does it mean to be educated and to have knowledge in the Systems Age? How are the two related, i.e., entertainment and knowledge? The questions seem basic, and yet strangely they have not even to our knowledge been asked let alone addressed.

TV news contains at least three central ingredients which work against its ability to treat reality cogently. First, the anchors have become celebrities themselves. This means, as illustrated by the George Bush/Dan Rather flap during the early days of the 1988 presidential campaign, that the news anchors are a constant threat to take precedence over the news itself. In many cases, they *are* the news. The millions of dollars (literally) they receive, the wacky incidents that happen to them, have become "news" in itself.[17]

Second, TV news is primarily big business. The bucks at stake are too high to consider news a public service. In the words of Van Gordon Sauter, former president of CBS News:

> "If I hear the words 'public trust' one more time, I think I'll shoot someone."[18]

Sauter would...be given credit for coining the term "infotainment," which even if he didn't invent it,he should have. A blend of information and entertainment was the essence of Sauter's take on television be it sports or news. When he was a news director in Chicago, he and his boss commissioned a designer to create a working news room for WBBM that could also be used as the studio set. They wanted desks, TV monitors, maps, water machines—all the stuff and noise of shirt-sleeve journalism—right there on camera. It was journalism as theater, and it worked; it was emulated at stations around the country.

The choice of Sauter as president of CBS News promised to help the cause of Dan Rather and a sagging rating; it also promised a generally interesting epic for CBS News—a place where the mere thought of news-as-entertainment was expressly against the rules. *The truth is, news can be sold to viewers like soap, and Van Sauter knew it* [italics ours]. That was why, in the early weeks of 1982, television screens across America were suddenly filled with an artful rendering of Dan Rather's darkly earnest face, etched in black against a grey background, and below it the legend:

> Our news organization sets the standards of excellence in television journalism. One journalist is the nation's leading anchorman. Together, they bring you the best evening news broadcast in America. Experienced. Trusted. Responsive. See the "CBS Evening News" with Dan Rather. See the difference, the best remains unchanged.

Over and over, day after day and night after night, that message was hammered out, in prime time and fringe time in long versions and short, always with the same payoff

theme—"The best remains unchanged." It was a mar-
velously effective promotion, simple and spare, almost
classical in its tones.[19]

This leads us to our last concern and/or recommenda-
tion. As we have said, we believe that a fundamental aspect
of the problem is both moral and ethical. In this light, it is a
sad commentary indeed that so-called great institutions
such as MIT, supported with the funding of some of
society's largest entertainment and news organizations,
have underwritten a media lab that is devoted primarily to
the explosion of the technology that will aid the unreality
industry.

We have no objection to the development of the technology per se, for as we have pointed out the same technology
that is capable of serving unreality is also capable of
serving complex reality. But shouldn't MIT have at least
one full-time person on its staff at the media lab whose job
is to explore the moral and ethical aspects of its inventions?
Or as is so typical of the case with a technological institution in a technologically fixated society, are such moral
ruminations to be left to themselves, or for a few "irrelevant ethicists" to ponder? Can we leave such concerns aside
when the problem we are facing is profoundly moral?

To say that the problem we are facing is profoundly
moral is in the end to face one of the more profoundly
depressing considerations of all. Noted peace activist
William Sloan Coffin once remarked that social movements succeed only when they have two important ingredients going for them:

— Moral clarity of purpose
— The existence of a group of people who are clearly
  affected by some clear social wrong

Thus, no matter how long it would take, blacks, women,
and gays were destined to succeed in righting the wrongs
committed against them for centuries. But who is clearly
wronged by unreality? Except for young children that
parents can contend legitimately are harmed by the Satur-

day morning TV cartoon shows, the wrong of unreality is so general as to be nonexistent. It affects everyone and therefore no one in particular. Further, it is linked up with one of our society's most central beliefs, that technology is the salvation to most of our problems. Therefore, until the problem or issue becomes severely or palpably clear, no action will be forthcoming, for no problem will be perceived.

In the final analysis, the problem of how to counter unreality is a problem of and for our whole culture. Our preoccupation with unreality is not due only to the complex nature of reality itself, to our unique cultural history, and to our current demise of leaders. We are preoccupied with unreality precisely because we lack a good myth, i.e., a really good Big Story to give ultimate meaning and purpose to our lives. The old myths, the old stories, have collapsed and no new ones have emerged to fill the vacuum.

It is only fitting that at the end of our investigation we can more adequately diagnose our situation than we could have at the beginning. The diagram on the following page identifies the situation as best we can describe it at this time. It says that there are four critical factors that govern a society's or culture's balancing of the forces that pull it towards reality versus unreality. *If* a genuinely adequate set of cultural myths are lacking to give meaning, direction, and purpose to people's lives, and further, *if* there is a vacuum of leadership to give voice to that mythology, i.e., to make it live, *then* given a reality that is too painful to bear, the people will drift towards unreality. Great, true leaders and myths are therefore necessary to stem the tide.

The fact of the matter is that the U.S. today lacks a true purpose to give meaning to people's lives. There are no shared, grand causes for which we are fighting. Furthermore, we still seem sapped by the tragic deaths of Jack and Robert Kennedy, and Martin Luther King. Their deaths, which were supposed to be the crisis to galvanize us, only stilled our idealism. And then came Vietnam and Watergate, which deliverd the final blows. As a result, belief in government and indeed all institutions continues to

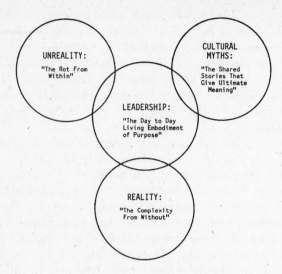

Figure 1. The Four Forces.

plummet. When there are no great causes or institutions into which we can invest our energies, then perhaps it is only inevitable that our energies should go into personal greed as had been the case during the Reagan years.

In the end, the questions facing us are: Have we become so satisfied with mediocrity, with mindless entertainment, with a second-rate educational system, that we no longer have the will to face reality directly? Are we prepared as a society to undertake the honest, hard work that it truly takes to live in a complex world?

Until we come to see that unreality affects not only our economic survival but our general well being, we shall drift from one enticing diversion to another:

[Says Robert Zemeckis, director of the film *Who Framed Roger Rabbit?*, human casting proved tricky.] To his surpirse, many great actors couldn't pull off the illusion; others simply weren't interested in sharing top billing with a rabbit. Then Bob Hoskins's name came up...says Zemeckis, "He made *me* believe Roger was actually there."

In a way, he was. "I had to build a relationship with thin air—to actually hallucinate that Roger was there," says

[Hoskins], who prepared for his role by watching his toddler daughter, Rose, play with an invisible friend. By the end of the exhausting five-month live-action shoot in London and Los Angeles, Hoskins began to lose control: "I was living with Toons day and night, and I actually began to see weasels sitting across from me at restaurants. The hallucinations began to take over."

[According to Zemeckis,] "Cartoon characters really do exist in the real world."

The phrase became a mantra for the marketing of *Roger Rabbit*. But Disney had to devise a campaign strategy that would hit movie goers of all ages. Ads target adults with a teasing "A man, a woman and a rabbit" copy line. The merchandise ranges from cuddly stuffed animals to sexy satin Jessica jackets. The Coca-Cola tie-in promotes the Yuppiefied diet version, while McDonalds is using Roger to hype not Happy Meals but special teenager-size sodas. Moreover, Disney has been trying to keep expectations low, thereby hoping to avoid a repeat of *Howard the Duck...*" We knew that audiences were going to be skeptical," says Disney Worldwide Marketing President Robert Levin. "Their attitude will be, 'Don't tell me cartoon characters are real. Show me.'"

The filmmakers have. Whether the film works on other levels, it achieves what Zemeckis set out to do—"To take two cinematic forms and stretch them to their limits." ... Zemeckis and company were willing to make the trek—proving along the way that Hollywood still will go to any length to entertain.[20]

Epilogue
A Fable

Adam—A Frankenstein or a Pinocchio for Our Times

...The adventure is always and everywhere a passage beyond the veil of the known into the unknown; the powers that watch at the boundary are dangerous; to deal with them is risky; yet for anyone with competence and courage the danger fades.

—Joseph Campbell, *The Hero With 1000 Faces*, Bollingen Series XV, Princeton, NJ: Princeton University Press, 1949, p. 82.

Adam Tate (or "AT" as he was called by his friends) woke quickly. It was Saturday, his favorite day of the week. Saturday meant playing baseball with the neighborhood gang.

To say that Adam or AT was popular was putting it

mildly. For one, he was easily the best player on the team. That was enough to make anyone a regular guy. But even more for all his skill AT was never flashy. He never grandstanded, bragged, or showed off. In short, Adam was an all around pleasant, nice kid in every way; he was good, but not "too good"; he was quiet, but not "overly quiet."

However, one always sensed that there was something— one could never quite put one's finger on it—that set AT apart and made him different, special, from the other kids. It came out in strange and odd ways.

Adam was bright, very bright indeed, perhaps even close to genius. But even the term genius fails to do justice to the special kind of brightness or genius Adam possessed. Someone once differentiated between ordinary and magical geniuses. Ordinary geniuses are the kind about whom one says, "Oh yes; if I were only a hundred times brighter I could have thought of that and worked it all out." Magical geniuses on the other hand are of a totally different kind. Their thoughts and creations are so strangely different, beautiful, and even shocking that one couldn't explain in a million years, even if one tried, how they ever came up with their ideas. For example, Adam not only was the first kid in his class to solve the really hard algebra problems on his tests, but he always invented a new kind of problem out of the original test problem that was so strange and beautiful that most of the time his algebra teacher couldn't even understand the new one, let alone solve it.

More than baseball itself, the one thing Adam loved to do was to go to the nearby science museum on Saturday mornings with his father, a warm man who also happened to be a gifted scientist. Adam awoke this particular Saturday morning with an even greater anticipation than he had had in weeks. The science museum was opening a special exhibit on robots and machines that pretended to think in the same way that humans did.

It contained not only a set of historical pictures and illustrations of robots, machines, and computers that pretended to think from the past, but also several exhibits of current examples. The centerpiece was a glass case that contained what looked to be a man sawed in half, mounted on a platform. The bottom half of what would have been the man's lower torso was exposed in such a way that one could see what seemed to be a million wires of every conceivable size, shape, and color running in and out of the top half. Furthermore, as one walked around the exhibit, one could also see a small patch on the back of the robot's head that was clearly exposed showing all kinds of electronic parts and boards stuffed inside the robot's head. Strangest of all was the sign that was posted in front of the exhibit which read, "Are you really sure that what you're looking at is really a robot? Maybe it's a trick, an illusion. Can you ask a question of HAL [the computer in the film *2001—A Space Odyssey*] that can prove conclusively that he is only a robot?"

Adam asked HAL two questions: Whether he could solve some of the very same problems he (Adam) had had on his algebra test, and whether he could discover some more interesting problems that went beyond the original ones much as he (Adam) had done. To his amazement and shock, Adam had just barely gotten the first question out of his mouth when HAL come back not only with the solution Adam had thought of but with five more problems that Adam himself had never thought of. But what really shook Adam was that HAL had looked him straight in the eye and had said: "You're no challenge for me, boy; anything you can think of, I can think of better; your problem is that you don't think I'm real, but I know better, I know that I am." And what really scared Adam was that HAL had a sinister smile on his face when he said this.

Adam was bothered all day by what had happened in the science museum. He went to his neighborhood baseball game as usual but he couldn't keep his mind on the game. He struck out every time at bat. He made five errors, more than he had made all season, and his team had lost eight to zip, the worst they had ever done.

That night when Adam came home, his father and mother were not only worried about his state of mind, but were very angry with the museum for putting together part of an exhibit that would scare a small boy. But the worst was only beginning.

After dinner, Adam complained that he had a headache and was feverish. As a result, he went to bed early, and that night had the worst nightmare he had ever had. In the dream, HAL was taunting him. And he had the same devilish smile as when he had confronted Adam in the museum. HAL was saying to him, "You'll never figure out a question that will prove I'm a machine; indeed, how do you know that you're really human after all? Maybe *you're* the one that's really a robot, not me. How do you know right now that your 'body' is not in the process of being converted into a machine…and by me, HAL. I have powers such as you've never dreamed of, boy."

Adam awoke screaming with a panic, a fear, that he had never experienced before. His parents naturally rushed into his room and listened to his dream and tried to comfort him. His father said gently but firmly, "Adam, humans have one thing above all that no machine could ever have, a soul. This is the deepest part that each of us has that makes us what we are—a truly unique human being. No one else, not even an identical twin, could ever share and possess the exact same soul."

When he finally went back to sleep, Adam had a second dream. In it he had been in a terrible car accident. It wasn't, however, just any old car accident, but a really bad one. In fact, the accident was so bad that Adam's body had become quite mangled, and in order to save his life, the doctors had to virtually reconstruct his entire body out of mechanical and electronic parts. In effect, Adam had become the first human ever to be composed more of metal and electronic parts than of human ones. There were people in the dream with Adam that he couldn't identify, but they kept saying that to see him after his accident was to see a technological freak. Only bits of anything truly human survived intact, a piece of bone here, a patch of skin or leg there. Indeed, the only organ that somehow made it through the accident untouched was his brain. Not even his heart survived. It had to be replaced with the latest artificial one.

The characters in his dream kept saying that it was morally wrong to have kept Adam alive in this way, if indeed "alive" was even a proper description. Was he an experiment gone amuck? Was he the unnatural extension of technology so that in effect Adam had become the first totally artificial human—an intelligent robot? Had Adam become what no scientist could ever have created in his lab, an electromechanical boy with a human brain? In his dream, right after Adam gained consiousness following his accident and became aware of his condition, he knew he was about to engage in a struggle. Should he reclaim his body by converting all that had been reshaped by his doctors and technology back into human blood, flesh, and bone, or would all that was metal and machine and electronics within him convert that which was still human and alive into more metal and machine? An oracle much like one that his class had studied during World History appeared in the dream and said, "Nature is never really content to have man and machine coexist; it never has been and never will be an equal partnership. Nature thus sets a contest to see which will master which; that is the contest you are about to enter, young Adam."

In Adam's dream, there were two endings to the story, depending upon which, man or machine, was the stronger of the two.

The first version went like this: Over a period of months, the scientists and doctors that attended Adam began to notice something that was more than just a little peculiar. It was in fact downright strange and even horrifying. As they compared microscopic examinations of Adam's reconstructed body over time, they noticed that the electronic wires which composed the inert parts of him began to look almost biological, one dare say even human. It was as though wires were slowly being converted into or replaced by human blood vessels. No one dared say it aloud, and yet it was very clear that indeed this was what was happening.

The second version was that, over a period of time, the doctors and the scientists attending Adam began to notice something truly strange if not frightening. Those parts of Adam that were still human after his accident began to take on a metal and electronic cast. It was almost as though what was flesh and blood was turning into computer chips and wires so that, in effect, if the process continued, Adam would no longer be one-eighth person and seven-eighths robot, but, as in a geometric progression, he would eventually become a complete nonhuman, a robot. Everything, including his once human brain, would be converted into a machine. The dream ended abruptly with the question, "What do you want to be?"

Notes

Chapter 1

1. Richard Schickel, *Intimate Strangers, The Culture of Celebrity*, Garden City, NY: Doubleday & Company, 1985.
2. Neil Postman, *Amusing Ourselves to Death, Public Discourse in the Age of Show Business*. New York: Viking, 1985.
3. Joshua Meyrowitz, *No Sense of Place, The Impact of Electronic Media on Social Behavior*, New York: Oxford University Press, 1985.
4. Allan Bloom, *The Closing of The American Mind, How Higher Education Has Failed Democracy and Impoverished the Souls of Today's Students*, New York: Simon & Schuster, 1987.
5. Irving Rein, Philip Kotler, and Martin Stoller, *High Visibility, How Executives, Politicians, Entertainers, Athletes, and Other Professionals Create, Market, and Achieve Successful Images*, New York: Dodd, Mead & Company, 1987, p. 68.
6. Dennis Farney, "Different Worlds, Main Street's View of the Crash Is Far From Wall Street's," *Wall Street Journal*, December 30, 1987, p. 10.

7. Stewart Brand, *The Media Lab, Inventing the Future at MIT.* New York: Viking, 1987.

8. Gary Wills, *Reagan's America, Innocence At Home*, Garden City, NY: Doubleday & Company, 1987.

9. Debora Silverman, *Selling Culture, Bloomingdale's Diana Vreeland, and The New Aristocracy of Taste in Reagan's America,* New York: Pantheon Books, 1986.

10. James D. Foley, "Interfaces for Advanced Computing," *Scientific American*, October 1987, pp. 126-135.

11. Brand, *op. cit.*

12. The number of pertinent references to television are by now so numerous that no one could hope to list all the relevant sources for this or any other chapter, let alone a whole book. The reader is merely referred to the following for an introduction:

   Jeffrey B. Abramson, F. Christopher Arterton, and Gary R. Orren, *The Electronic Commonwealth, the Impact of New Media Technologies on Democratic Politics,* New York: Basic Books, 1988.

   Todd Gitlin (Ed.), *Watching Television*, New York: Pantheon Books, 1986.

   Elihu Katz and Tamas Szecsko (Eds.), *Mass Media and Social Change*, Beverly Hills, CA: Sage, 1981.

   Martin Linsky, *Impact, How the Press Affects Federal Policy Making.* New York: Norton, 1986.

   Martin Mayer, *Making News.* Garden City, NY: Doubleday and Company, 1987.

   Margaret Morse, "The Television News Personality and Credibility: Reflection on the News in Transition," in Tania Modleski (Ed.), *Studies in Entertainment, Critical Approaches to Mass Culture*, Bloomington, IN: Indiana University Press, 1986, pp. 55-79.

   Martin Schram, *The Great American Video Game, Presidential Politics in The Television Age*, New York: William Morrow, 1987.

13. Diane Haithman, "CBS' 'Forty-Eight Hours' Hopes to Break Down Barriers," *Los Angeles Times*, January 19, 1988, pp. 1 and 3.

14. Jay Sharbutt, "The State of the Network News Business, Despite Declining Ratings, Increasing Competition, Counter-Programming and Shifting Time Slots, The Evening Newscasts Are Far From Extinct," *Los Angeles Times*, December 28, 1987, p. 1; Dennis McDougal, "Broadcast

News, L.A.," *Los Angeles Times Magazine,* January 24, 1988, pp. 6-17.

15. See especially the essay by Daniel C. Hallin, "We Keep America on Top of the World," in Todd Gitlin (Ed.), *Watching Television.* New York: Pantheon Books, 1986, pp. 9-41.

16. Louis Harris, *Inside America.* New York: Vintage Books, 1987.

17. Howard Rosenberg, "And Now, Let's Hail the Messengers Who Bring Us News on Channel 2," *Los Angeles Times,* January 6, 1988, p. 1 and 9.

18. For an in-depth discussion of various philosophical systems and particularly on the notion of a guarantor and how it differs from philosophical system to system, see C. West Churchman's, *The Design of Inquiring Systems.* New York: Basic Books, 1971; see also Ian I. Mitroff, "Systems, Inquiry, and the Meanings of Falsification," *Philosophy of Science,* Volume 40, No. 2, June 1973, pp. 255-276.

19. Were Meyrowitz, *op.cit.,* conversant with the langage of a guarantor, he might say that different media have different guarantors. Thus, in Meyrowitz's terms the guarantor of TV is its ability to capture the emotional expressiveness that is distinctive of human beings. In other words, TV's guarantor *is* emotional expressiveness. On the other hand, the guarantor of print media, e.g., books, *is* the logical coherency of an argument, etc.

20. Ian I. Mitroff, *The Subjective Side of Science, A Philosophical Inquiry into the Psychology of the Apollo Moon Scientists.* Amsterdam: Elsevier, 1974.

21. Carol Tavris, *Los Angeles Times,* November 1, 1987, p. 5.

22. David Remnick, "Good News Is No News," *Esquire,* October 1987, p. 158.

23. Richard Zoglin, "Get Ready for McRather," *Time,* April 11, 1988.

Chapter 2

1. For a fuller understanding of the points discussed in this chapter, the reader is referred to a previous book by the first author, *Business Not as Usual, Rethinking Our Individual, Corporate, and Industrial Strategies for Global Competition,* San Francisco, CA: Jossey-Bass, 1987; see also Ian I. Mitroff, "The Complete and Utter Failure of Traditional

Thinking in Comprehending the Nuclear Dilemma: Why It's Impossible to Formulate a Paradox-Free Theory of Nuclear Strategy," *Journal of Technological Forecasting and Social Change*, 1986, *29*, pp. 51-72.

2. I.C. Magaziner and Robert B. Reich, *Minding America's Business, The Decline and Rise of the American Economy*. New York: Vintage, 1983.

3. Marvin Harris, *Why Nothing Works, The Anthropology of Daily Life*. New York: Touchstone, 1981.

4. The reader is referred to the earlier paper by Mitroff, *op.cit.*, for an in-depth discussion of the paradoxes which haunt nuclear phenomena and increasingly all phenomena which are global.

5. *Business Week*, December 22, 1986.

6. Paul Shrivastava, *Bhopal: Anatomy of a Disaster*. New York: Harper & Row, 1987.

7. Stewart Brand, *The Media Lab, Inventing the Future at MIT*. New York: Viking, 1987.

Chapter 3

1. Roland Marchand, *Advertising the American Dream, Making Way for Modernity, 1920-1940*. Berkeley, CA: University of California Press, 1985, p. 106.

2. Marchand, *op.cit.*, p. 115.

3. For an important examination of the role that sound plays in television and the notion of reverse causality that it engenders, see Rick Altman, "Television/Sound," in Tania Modleski (ED.), *Studies in Entertainment, Critical Approaches to Mass Culture*, Bloomington, IN: Indiana University Press, 1986, pp. 39-54.

4. See Jeffrey C. Alexander, "The Mass News Media in Systemic, Historical, and Comparative Perspective," in *Mass Media and Social Change*, Elihu Katz and Tamas Szecsko (Eds.). Beverly Hills, CA: Sage, 1981, pp. 17-51; see also, Joshua Meyrowitz, *No Sense of Place, The Impact of Electronic Media on Social Behavior*, New York: Oxford University Press, 1985, for a masterful account of the general phenomenon of the blurring between traditional boundaries as the result of the widespread impact of TV on our general culture; in addition, see Margaret Morse, "The Television News Personality and Credibility: Reflection on the News in Transition," in Tania Modleski (Ed.),

Studies in Entertainment, Critical Approaches to Mass Culture, Bloomington, IN: Indiana University Press, 1986, pp. 55-79, for another excellent treatment of the phenomenon of Boundary Warping.

5. See the generally excellent essay by Pat Aufderheide, "Music Videos: The Look of the Sound," in Todd Gitlin (Ed.) *Watching Television*. New York: Pantheon Books, 1986, pp. 111-135.

6. Marsha Kinder, "Music Video and the Spectator: Television, Ideology and Dream": *Film Quarterly*, Fall 1984, pp. 2-15.

7. See Aufderheide, *op.cit.*

8. *Ibid.*

9. *Ibid.*

10. *Ibid.*

11. *Ibid.*

12. *Ibid.*, p. 127.

13. Aufderheide, *op.cit.*

14. See Tom Engelhardt, "Children's Television: The Shortcake Strategy," in Todd Gitlin (Ed.) *Watching Television*. New York: Pantheon Books, 1986, pp. 68-110.

15. *Ibid.*

16. *Ibid.* p. 91.

17. *Ibid.*

18. See Michael Sorkin, "Simulations: Faking It," in Todd Gitlin (Ed.) *Watching Television*. New York: Pantheon Books, 1986, pp. 162-182.

19. Meyrowitz, *op.cit.*

Chapter 4

1. James Gleick, *Chaos, Making a New Science*. New York: Viking, 1987.

2. See Ruth Rosen, "Soap Operas: Search for Yesterday," in Todd Gitlin (Ed.) *Watching Television*. New York: Pantheon Books, 1986, pp. 42-67.

3. *Ibid.*, p. 45.

4. *Ibid.*, p. 50.

5. *Ibid.*

6. *Ibid.*, p. 61.

7. Robert N. Bellah, et al., *Habits of the Heart: Individualism and Commitment in American Life*. Berkeley, CA: University of California Press, 1985; and Jackson Lears, *No Place of*

Grace, *Antimodernism in the Transformation of American Culture 1880-1920*. New York: Pantheon Books, 1981.

8. *Ibid.*

9. J. Martin, *Who Am I This Time? Uncovering the Fictive Personality*. New York: Norton, 1988.

10. *Ibid.*

11. Irving Rein, Philip Kotler, and Martin Stoller, *High Visibility, How Executives, Politicians, Entertainers, Athletes, and Other Professionals Create, Market, and Achieve Successful Images*. New York: Dodd, Mead & Company, 1987, p. 68.

12. See James D. Foley, "Interfaces for Advanced Computing," *Scientific American*, October 1987, pp. 126-135.

13. Stewart Brand, *The Media Lab, Inventing the Future at MIT*. New York: Viking, 1987.

14. *Ibid.;* see also Mark Crispin Miller, "Prime Time: Deride and Conquer," in Todd Gitlin (Ed.) *Watching Television*. New York: Pantheon Books, 1986, pp. 183-228.

15. Neil Postman, *Amusing Ourselves to Death, Public Discourse in the Age of Show Business*. New York: Viking, 1985.

16. See Foley, *op.cit.*; see also Brand, *op.cit.*

17. Foley, *op.cit.*

18. David Zeltzer, quoted in Brand, *op.cit.*, p. 223.

Chapter 5

1. Irving J. Rein, Philip Kotler, and Martin R. Stoller, *High Visibility, How Executives, Politicians, Entertainers, Athletes, and Other Professionals Create, Market, and Achieve Successful Images*. New York: Dodd, Mead & Company, 1987.

2. Richard Schickel, *Intimate Strangers, The Culture of Celebrity, How Our National Obsession With Celebrity Shapes Our Worlds and Bends Our Minds*. Garden City, NY: Doubleday & Company, 1985.

3. Rein, et al., *op.cit.*, p. 29.

4. Neil Postman, *Amusing Ourselves to Death, Public Discourse in The Age of Show Business*. New York: Viking, 1985.

5. See Mitroff, *Breakaway Thinking, How to Analyze Your Business Assumptions (And Why You Should)*. New York: John Wiley & Sons, 1988.

6. Ian I. Mitroff and Ralph H. Kilmann, *Corporate Tragedies, Product Tampering, Sabotage, and Other Catastrophes*. New York: Praeger, 1984.

7. *Ibid.*

8. Mitroff, *Breakaway Thinking, op.cit.*

9. These figures are adopted from Rein, et al., *op.cit.*

10. Rein, et al., *High Visibility, op.cit.*, pp. 70-72.

11. *Ibid.*

12. *Ibid.*, 152-153.

13. Schickel, *op.cit.*

14. Leo Braudy, *The Frenzy of Renown, Fame and Its History,* New York: Oxford University Press, 1986.

15. *Ibid.*

16. *Ibid.*, p. 89.

17. *Ibid.*, p. 111.

18. Braudy, *op.cit.*

19. Howard Rosenberg, "The Rise and Fall of a Golden Anchor," *Los Angeles Times*, June 8, 1988, Part IV, pp. 1 & 10.

20. Steven Stack, "Celebrities and Suicide: A Taxonomy and Analysis, 1948-1983," *American Sociological Review*, 1987, Vol. 52 (June: pp. 401-412).

21. Rein, et al., *High Visibility*, p. 68.

22. Rein, et al., *High Visibility*, p. 30.

Chapter 6

1. Robert Ornstein, *Multi Mind, A New Way of Looking at Human Behavior.* Boston: Houghton Mifflin, 1986.

2. *Ibid.*, pp.25-28.

3. *Ibid.*, p. 160.

4. Portions of this section were drawn from a previously published work; see I.I. Mitroff, *Stakeholders of the Organizational Mind.* San Francisco: Jossey Bass, 1983.

5. J. Jacobi, *Complex/Archetypes/Symbol and The Psychology of C.G. Jung.* Bollingen Series 57, Princeton, NJ: Princeton University Press, 1959; C.G. Jung, *Four Archetypes, Mother/ Rebirth/Spirit/Trickster.* Princeton, NJ: Princeton University Press, 1973; see Mitroff, *op.cit.*

6. R. McCully, *Rorschach Theory & Symbolism, A Jungian Approach to the Clinical Material.* Baltimore, MD: Williams & Williams, 1971, p. 51.

7. B. Bettelheim, *The Uses of Enchantment: The Meaning and Importance of Fairy Tales.* New York: Vintage, 1977, pp. 8-9.

8. M. Milich, "The Wonderful Wizard of Ogdensburg: Robert Woodhead," *Softline*, Vol. 1, No. 4, 1982, p. 38.

9. *Op.cit.*, p. 38.

10. R.R. Adams, "Come Cast a Spell With Me," *Softline*, Vol. 1, No. 4, 1982, pp. 31-32.

11. Paul Moxnes, "Deep Roles: An Archetypal Model of Organizational Roles," working paper, presented at the Third Conference on Organizational Symbolism in Corporate Culture, Milano, Italy, June 26, 1987.

12. See Irving J. Rein, Philip Kotler, and Martin R. Stoller, *High Visibility, How Executives, Politicians, Entertainers, Athletes, and Other Professionals Create, Market, and Achieve Successful Images*. New York: Dodd, Mead & Company, 1987, p. 12.

13. Margaux Hemingway as told to senior writer Kristin McMurran, *People*, February 8, 1988, p. 96.

14. T. Jackson Lears, *No Place of Grace, Antimodernism and the Transformation of American Culture 1880-1920*. New York: Pantheon Book, 1981, p. 8.

15. *Ibid.*, p. 32.

16. James Fallows, "Japan: Playing by Different Rules, In the U.S. Economy the Consumer Is Sovereign; In the Japanese the Producer Is. It's a Fundamental Difference," *Atlantic Monthly*, September, 1987, pp. 22-32.

18. Loren Baritz, *Backfire, A History of How American Culture Led Us Into Vietnam and Made Us Fight the Way We Did*, New York: Ballantine Books, 1985, p. 249.

19. See Lears, *op.cit.*; although Lears' book is neither an explicit account of unreality in American history nor was it intentionally written as such, it nonetheless can be read as a fascinating historical account of the nature and development of American unreality over the period of history with which he deals.

Chapter 7

1. An earlier version of this essay appeared by Warren Bennis, *New Management*, November 1988.

2. Joseph Campbell, *The Hero With 1000 Faces*, Bollingen Series, Princeton University Press, 1968.

3. Alfred North Whitehead, quoted in *The Temporary Society*. New York: Harper & Row, 1968.

4. See Gary Wills, *Reagan's America, Innocence at Home*. Gorden City, NY: Doubleday & Company, 1985.

5. Debora Silverman, *Selling Culture, Bloomingdale's Diana Vreeland, and the New Aristocracy of Taste in Reagan's America*. New York: Pantheon Books, 1986.

6. See Campbell, *op. cit.*

7. See Wills, *op. cit.*

8. Robert N. Bella, et al., *Habits of the Heart: Individualism and Commitment in American Life*, Berkeley, CA: University of California Press, 1985.

9. Russell Jacoby, *The Last Intellectuals, American Culture in the Age of Academe*, New York, Basic Books, 1987.

10. *Ibid.*
    Ibid.

Chapter 8

1. Robert Shogan, "Little Else in Campaign to Focus On, Character Issue Shaping Strategy in Both Parties," *Los Angeles Times*, February 1, 1988, pp. 1 and 13.

2. Stephen Weinstein, "Alf: The Star Trek of NBC's Furry Resident Alien, How a Wisecracking Puppet Toddled Into the Hearts of Viewers," *Los Angeles Times*, December 23, 1987, p. 1 and 10.

3. Peter Tasker, *The Japanese, A Major Exploration of Modern Japan*, New York: E.P. Dutton, 1987, pp. 131-132.

4. C. West Churchman, *Thought and Wisdom*, Seaside, CA: Intersystems Press, 1983; and *The Design of Inquiring Systems*, New York: Basic Books, 1971.

5. See Mitroff, et al., *Business Not As Usual, Rethinking Our Individual, Corporate, and Industrial Strategies for Global Competition*, Jossey-Bass, San Francisco, 1988; and, *Break-Away Thinking, How to Challenge Your Business Assumptions (And Why You Should)*, New York: John Wiley & Sons, 1988.

6. Benjamin Duke, *Lessons for Industrial America, The Japanese School.* New York: Praeger, 1986; Merry White, *The Japanese Educational Challenge, A Commitment to Children.* New York: The Free Press, 1987.

7. Joshua Meyrowitz, *No Sense of Place, The Impact of Electronic Media on Social Behavior.* New York: Oxford University Press, 1985.

8. Neil Postman, *Amusing Ourselves to Death: Public Discourse in the Age of Show Business.* New York: Viking, 1985.

9. Robert Reich, *Tales of a New America.* New York: Times Books, 1987.

10. Marshall McLuhan, *The Gutenberg Galaxy.* Toronto: University of Toronto Press, 1962.

11. See Duke, and White, *op.cit.*

12. Russell Jacoby, *The Last Intellectuals, American Culture in the Age of Academe*. New York: Basic Books, 1987.
13. Nikki Finke, "A Fantasy Named Danielle Steel, After Twenty-Three Books in Fifteen Years, Her World Sometimes Seems Too Unreal to Be True," *Los Angeles Times,* January 6, 1988, p. 1 and 4.
14. Shirley MacLaine, *Out on a Limb*. New York: Bantam Books, 1983, pp. 199-213.
15. This is also where we part company with Joshua Meyrowitz, *op.cit.* There is much in Meyrowitz's general thesis and arguments with which we agree strongly. If we part company, it is only with regard to those properties of TV that are truly those of "the medium itself" and those which are rather the result of a highly complex interplay between "the medium," the unique psychological makeup of humans, and the particular properties of American culture that have both shaped TV and in turn have been shaped by it. In other words, we see the equation of influence as much more complex than does Meyrowitz. Nonetheless, we agree with many if not most of his highly perceptive observations of what the medium itself has done to warp and blur many of the boundaries between disciplines, professions, and realms of our lives.
16. W. Russell Neuman, *The Paradox of Mass Politics, Knowledge and Opinion in the American Electorate*. Cambridge, MA: Harvard University Press, 1986.
17. Peter Boyer, "Broadcast Blues," *Vanity Fair,* January 1988, pp. 62-68, pp. 109-114.
18. *Ibid.*, p. 113.
19. *Ibid.*, pp. 109-110.
20. Michael Reese, "The Making of Roger Rabbit, Disney and Spielberg Mix Actors and Cartoon Characters on a 45 Million Dollar Gamble," *Newsweek,* June 27, 1988, pp. 58-59.

Index